A Georgetown Life

A Georgetown Life

THE REMINISCENCES OF

Britannia Wellington Peter Kennon

OF TUDOR PLACE

Grant S. Quertermous

Georgetown University Press / Washington, DC

The publisher is not responsible for third-party websites or their content. URL links were active at time of publication.

Library of Congress Cataloging-in-Publication Data

Names: Kennon, Britannia Wellington Peter, 1815-1911, author. | Quertermous, Grant, editor, author.
Title: A Georgetown Life : The Reminiscences of Britannia Wellington Peter Kennon of Tudor Place / Grant Quertermous.
Other titles: Reminiscences of Britannia Kennon of Tudor Place
Description: Washington, DC : Georgetown University Press, 2020. | Includes bibliographical references and index.
Identifiers: LCCN 2020008233 | ISBN 9781647120412 (hardcover) | ISBN 9781647120429 (ebook)
Subjects: LCSH: Kennon, Britannia Wellington Peter, 1815-1911. | Kennon, Britannia Wellington Peter, 1815-1911—Family. | Tudor Place (Washington, D.C.)—History. | Women—Washington (D.C.)—Biography. | Washington (D.C.)—Biography. | Georgetown (Washington, D.C.)—History. | Washington (D.C.)—History.
Classification: LCC F202.G3 K46 2020 | DDC 975.3/02092 [B]—dc23
LC record available at https://lccn.loc.gov/2020008233

This book is printed on acid-free paper meeting the requirements of the American National Standard for Permanence in Paper for Printed Library Materials.

21 20   9 8 7 6 5 4 3 2 First printing

Printed in the United States of America
Designed by Erin Kirk

Contents

Illustrations

Acknowledgments

Any scholarly endeavor relies on many factors wholly separate from the author's ability to digest, analyze, and synthesize a large body of historical evidence. Other key ingredients are the availability of good primary source material as well as the assistance of knowledgeable and talented individuals in all steps of the process from research to editing and, finally, to publication. There are many people to whom I'm indebted for their assistance, suggestions, or expertise in some aspect of this project over the past 2 years, although I also want to acknowledge those who have played a part in this project over the past 125 years.

This book would not have been possible without the efforts of Britannia W. Kennon's grandchildren, who "interviewed" her in the late nineteenth century and prompted her to share memories as well as her encyclopedic knowledge of Custis-Peter family genealogy that is presented in this volume. It was Armistead Peter Jr. who principally undertook these efforts with the help of his siblings Agnes Peter and Rev. Dr. G. Freeland Peter. The contributions of Britannia's grandson Walter G. Peter should also be recognized, as he compiled his own reminiscences later in his life that included important information about his grandmother as well as transcriptions of family letters, obituaries, and other

important information that served as a key resource for this project. Each of these grandchildren also did their part to preserve the archive of significant family papers, which they received after Britannia's death in 1911. The subsequent generations further enabled the preservation of these important papers by ensuring that they ended up in repositories where they could be preserved and used by scholars.

I'm grateful to Armistead Peter 3rd, who had the vision to create a foundation, now called the Tudor Place Foundation, to share with the public an amazing house and unparalleled family collection representing five generations of the Peter family. For the thirty-two years that Tudor Place has been open as a historic house museum, Britannia Kennon's documented reminiscences have been the Rosetta Stone that divulged clues about the house and its two centuries of history. The information provided by Britannia and then recorded by her grandchildren guided the interpretation of the house from the day the museum opened and still continues to influence how the house is presented to visitors.

I also want to recognize the efforts of previous Tudor Place staff members and volunteers over the past three decades, who transcribed excerpts from the manuscript we refer to as Britannia's Reminiscences or conducted detailed research on a topic she discussed. These people included Eleanor Preston, Judy Frank, Melinda Linderer Huff, Bertha Kuniholm, Osborne P. Mackie, and Erin Kuykendall Thomas. Additional research focused on enslaved and domestic servants at Tudor Place was compiled by Anne Webb and Ann King as part of the Tudor Place Domestic Service Research Project between 2002 and 2004, and by Mary Beth Corrigan, who authored several reports focused on slavery at Tudor Place as well as the larger African American community in Georgetown as part of a 2012–13 project made possible by a grant from the DC Humanities Council.

I could not have completed this project without the support of my colleagues at Tudor Place Historic House and Garden, where I have had the privilege of serving as curator since 2015. The idea for this book, an annotated and accessible version of Britannia's Reminiscences, was the result of a conversation I had in the fall of 2017 with Hillary Rothberg, director of education and visitor services. I'm grateful to executive director Mark Hudson for his encouragement throughout this undertaking and for the support of the foundation's board of trustees. Bryn Cooley, collections manager, reviewed drafts of both of my essays and offered valuable editorial and critical feedback. Artist-in-residence Peter Waddell assisted by taking photographs of some of the objects that are used as illustrations. Finally, I want to recognize longtime Tudor Place archivist Wendy Kail, whose essays and *Tudor Place Times* newsletter articles provided valuable contextual information and further aided in identifying people mentioned by Britannia in some of the sections of the manuscript.

Today portions of the Peter Family Archive reside in three repositories. In addition to the papers now found in the Tudor Place Archives, a portion of the family collection is now housed in the Fred W. Smith National Library for the Study of George Washington at Mount Vernon, and another portion of the Peter family papers are located at the Albert and Shirley Small Special Collections Library at the University of Virginia. I want to acknowledge the assistance of the staff at both of these institutions for providing access to these papers from which I've quoted or cited in my essays and footnotes.

I'm also grateful to a number of colleagues in other institutions who directed me to important primary and secondary sources during the course of the project as well as several individuals who shared information or excerpts from their own unpublished work that directly benefited my project. Cassandra Good, assistant professor of history at Marymount University, generously shared several research discoveries and offered valuable insight gleaned from her own project, a biography of the Custis grandchildren, during the time I was working on this project. Joseph Mannard, professor of history at Indiana University of Pennsylvania, generously shared his own research about Ann Gertrude Wightt, the former nun who lived for a time at Tudor Place after renouncing her vows and leaving Georgetown's Visitation Convent in 1831.

My project also greatly benefited from assistance provided by colleagues from other institutions related to the Custis and Washington families. At Mount Vernon, I want to thank Adam Erby as well as Dawn Bonner,

Amanda Isaac, Jessie MacLeod, Elisabeth Malin, and Samantha Snyder; at Woodlawn, Amanda Phillips and her staff; and at the George Washington Foundation, Meghan Budinger and Jessica Burger.

Other individuals I want to thank include Leslie Buhler, Erin Beasley, Conna Clark, Nichol Gabor, Matthew Gilmore, Jackie Killian, Jerry McCoy, David McKenzie, Susan Nalezyty, LuLen Walker, and Virginia Velez as well as Al Bertrand and his staff at Georgetown University Press.

I also want to think my parents, Steven and Vicky Quertermous, who encouraged me to nurture a love of history and an appreciation for the past by filling my childhood with vacations that involved antiquing and visits to historic sites and museums, all of which helped me to find a career field and job that I truly love as the curator of a historic house museum.

Finally, my wife, Katie Quertermous, not only offered endless encouragement but also read over this entire manuscript and very patiently dealt with my tendency to overuse commas by removing them when they were unnecessary and, in several instances, adding them when they were absent. Our son, Caleb, was born during the conclusion of this project, and I have enjoyed making many of the final revisions while holding him as he happily slept in my arms.

A Georgetown Life

Capturing Memories to Preserve a Family's History

As the dawn of the twentieth century approached, Britannia Wellington Peter Kennon (1815–1911) was nearing her eighty-fifth birthday. A lifelong resident of both Tudor Place and the Georgetown neighborhood of Washington, DC, Britannia bore witness to many of the significant events that occurred in and around the nation's capital over the course of her lifetime. Britannia's grandchildren, the four sons and daughter of Martha Custis Kennon Peter and Dr. Armistead Peter, recognized the importance of their grandmother as a source of collective family history and living link to their Calvert, Custis, and Washington ancestry. Through her mother, Martha Parke Custis Peter, Britannia was a great-granddaughter of First Lady Martha Washington; she lived her life surrounded by the family's sizable and significant collection of furniture, table wares, manuscripts, and engravings that were once owned by President and Mrs. Washington. Britannia Kennon's nine-decade residency in Georgetown gave her ample opportunity to interact with numerous historical and political figures while she worked to preserve the Tudor Place property and this unique collection of Custis-Washington family heirlooms.

Starting in 1894, Britannia's grandchildren began prompting her to share recollections of past events as well as her vast knowledge of family history. As she spoke, they began to write, capturing the information and the memories, exactly as she recounted them. The compilation of their notes from these conversations form the manuscript known as "Britannia Kennon's Reminiscences," which is now found in the Tudor Place Archives. This undertaking allowed the Peter grandchildren to commit to paper the stories they had grown up hearing from their grandmother, such as her description of Lafayette's 1824 visit to Tudor Place and her time as a pupil at Georgetown's Young Ladies Academy—known today as Georgetown Visitation Preparatory School. More tumultuous memories are also described in her recollections, such as her decision to take in Union officers as boarders during the Civil War in an effort to prevent Tudor Place from being seized by the federal government for use as a hospital. In addition to her own memories and experiences, Britannia shared with her grandchildren additional anecdotes that were passed on to her by her mother, Martha Peter. This information, recounted second-hand, included details of Martha's childhood visits to

Mount Vernon and of accompanying President George Washington to the September 18, 1793, laying of the cornerstone of the United States Capitol Building. This information, originally conveyed to Britannia and then retold by her to her grandchildren, further illuminates how George and Martha Washington were perceived and memorialized by later generations of their family—including Britannia's five grandchildren.

Britannia served as a beloved maternal figure to her grandchildren, particularly following the death of their own mother in 1886. The Peter siblings ranged in age from eighteen to six years old when Martha "Markie" Custis Kennon Peter died suddenly on September 8, 1886. Even as her grandchildren matured, reached adulthood, and moved away from Tudor Place, Britannia remained an important part of their lives and someone with whom they frequently corresponded and visited.

When her grandchildren began these conversations in 1894, Britannia Kennon was seventy-nine years old and the only surviving great-grandchild of Martha Washington. Several years prior, in May 1890, an article about Britannia and her collection of Washington heirlooms at Tudor Place had been published in the *Century Monthly Illustrated Magazine*.[1] The article not only illustrated many of the Custis-Washington objects then in Britannia's possession but also contained anecdotes and information about George and Martha Washington originally recounted to Britannia by her mother, Martha Custis Peter. A second article also published in the *Century Magazine* in 1892 by art historian Charles Henry Hart focused on the portraits and portrait miniatures of the Washingtons then in Britannia's possession.[2] In the summer of 1893 Britannia was also an invited guest to Virginia Day to attend the World's Columbian Exposition in Chicago.

Britannia's grandson Armistead Peter Jr. (referred to as Armistead Jr. to avoid confusion with both his father and his son who shared the same name) was the primary force in ensuring that his grandmother's recollections were preserved for later generations of the family. A majority of the notes recording these stories and facts were written by him. In some instances they are carefully written out in a lined notebook; in other instances they are jotted down on scraps of whatever piece of paper was close at hand, including the back of a deposit slip from a local Washington bank. Other surviving examples are in the hand of Agnes Peter Mott or G. Freeland Peter, Armistead Jr.'s two youngest siblings, who lived with Britannia at Tudor Place until the time of her 1911 death. In addition to his role as the unofficial family historian, Armistead Jr. followed his grandmother's example of adding small notes or labels to important objects in the family's collection to provide insight on their provenance or source. And, like his grandmother, Armistead Jr. also compiled his own reminiscences in the mid-twentieth century after he reached old age. His reminiscences contain additional stories and information passed along to him by his grandmother as well as by his father, Dr. Armistead Peter, a prominent Georgetown physician.[3]

Britannia recognized her grandson's interest in family history and frequently gave him objects or manuscripts from the family collection as well as bundles of old family papers that were tucked away in corners of the Tudor Place attic. Later in life Armistead Jr. recalled that "because of my interest in family matters, grandmother gave me a trunkful of old papers that were at Tudor." He went on to note that Britannia said he "was the only one that took the slightest interest in them and she knew that they would be preserved and cared for by me."[4] Armistead Jr. similarly received another large trunk, this time from his father, filled with letters and documents that had originally been inherited by Thomas Peter in 1806 after the death of his own father, the family patriarch, Robert Peter.

In an 1895 letter to Armistead Jr. when he was newly married and living in New York City, Britannia wrote that she wished that he was seated by her in the Tudor Place parlor and they "could talk over so many things of interest to us both."[5] Each time Armistead Jr. returned to Georgetown to visit his grandmother, he continued to conduct oral history interviews with her. His diary entry of April 9, 1897, typical of these visits, notes that he "read over some papers with Grandma on family history."[6] After spending the day with her on May 13, 1899, he confided to his diary his desire to "write down all that she tells me of the past. A most interesting volume it would make."[7]

Armistead Jr. carefully preserved the notes from his conversations with his grandmother, and today they are found within his personal papers in the Tudor Place Archives. Armistead Jr.'s papers occupy a total of seventy-five linear feet of space in the archives and illustrate his habit of retaining all manner of ephemera, receipts, canceled checks, and both business and personal correspondence. He kept a daily diary for much of his lifetime, the early volumes of which are filled with mentions of the time he spent sitting and talking with his grandmother or conducting research on some aspect of the family's history. Also found within his papers are notes from supplemental historical and genealogical research that he had undertaken, including files of family birth and death records that he copied from a distant relative's Bible and a list of the entries in the published *Diaries of George Washington* that mention his great-grandparents Thomas and Martha Peter. Armistead Jr.'s interest in family history led him to use a copy of *Burke's Landed Gentry* to identify and locate collateral Peter family members in Scotland as potential sources for his research on earlier generations of the family prior to Robert Peter's immigration to Maryland in 1746.

In the late nineteenth century, when Armistead Jr. was interviewing his grandmother and most actively engaged in his research on the family's history, there were few public repositories to house historical records; thus, both his grandmother's memory and the collection of Peter family papers at Tudor Place were valuable and accessible research tools for his project. Prior to her 1911 death and the division of her estate, Britannia possessed a large collection of family papers, including the only two extant letters from George to Martha Washington known at that time as well as letters of condolence received by Mrs. Washington at the time of President Washington's death from President John Adams and other former members of the first president's administration. Since Britannia's father, Thomas Peter, served as one of the executors of Martha Washington's estate, the family archive also held important documents about the settlement of the estate and an account of the 1802 sale at Mount Vernon identifying the buyers of each item sold. The family papers additionally contained records from Thomas and Martha Peter's purchase of Tudor Place and papers from Britannia's own lifetime, such as bills paid by her father for her school tuition and letters from her elder sisters written from New York and Philadelphia.

Even as early as the second decade of the nineteenth century, the Peter family's collection of Custis-Washington papers at Tudor Place was an important resource for historians engaged in conducting historical or biographical research on George and Martha Washington. As Britannia described to her grandchildren, President Washington's nineteenth-century biographers Jared Sparks and Benson Lossing used letters or other documents in the Peter family's collection. Similarly, they spoke with Martha Custis Peter to hear firsthand her recollections of her stepgrandfather and details of his personality and daily routine. Sparks recounted his February 28, 1828, visit to Tudor Place in his diary, summarizing the conversation he had with Martha Peter about Martha Washington's decision to burn much of President Washington's personal correspondence after his death and how Mrs. Peter found two surviving letters behind a drawer of Mrs. Washington's writing table.[8]

In contrast to this archive of family papers and objects that Britannia possessed and encouraged her grandson to use for his research in the 1890s, the bulk of George Washington's correspondence was not publicly accessible during this time period, as it was held by the State Department. Originally purchased from George Corbin Washington, the president's grandnephew, the personal papers and diaries as well as the state papers from Washington's administration were not transferred to the Library of Congress until 1904.[9] As part of the library's institutional reorganization in 1897, The Manuscript Division was created to house important papers including those of former presidents after they came under the ownership of the federal government. In the city of Washington, the Historical Society of Washington, DC, existed but was in its infancy. Founded in 1894 as the Columbia Historical Society, its role at the time was to serve as a forum where its members presented papers of historical research, many of which were then published in its journal, *Records of the Columbia Historical Society*. Even the National Archives and Records Administration, now the primary federal governmental body charged with preserving and managing historical records, was not created until the 1930s. As Francesca Morgan writes in a 2010 *New England Quarterly* article, "Broadly accessible public libraries and archives are a relatively modern innovation."[10]

Up until the late twentieth century and the advent of census databases and online repositories used today for genealogical and historical records, individuals like Armistead Jr. who were conducting this type of research had to spend hours in courthouses searching probate records or visiting multiple churches and rectories to locate old vestry books and baptismal records. Birth and death records found in the leaves of family Bibles like Martha Peter's Bible, now in the Tudor Place Archives, acted as another important source. Britannia inherited her mother's Bible in 1854, and she continued to add family records to it, carefully noting every birth, marriage, or death of an immediate family member that occurred in her lifetime. In 1892 Armistead Jr. was given his great-great-grandfather Robert Peter's Bible, which contained birth records for Thomas Peter and his eleven siblings.

Another frequently used source for historical research was elderly members of a community who served as firsthand witnesses to a significant event. Many of the nineteenth-century histories of Washington, DC, and the articles that appear in the early volumes of the *Records of the Columbia Historical Society* contain the same type of personal recollections as those Britannia Kennon provided to her grandchildren. Unlike Washingtonians such as Christian Hines, Sally Somervell Mackall, or Marian Campbell Gouverneur, all of whom published memoirs of their life in nineteenth-century Washington, DC, Britannia appears to have had no interest in writing and publishing her memoir. She frequently granted interviews to local reporters to whom she recalled events like Lafayette's visit, but everything of a historical nature that she wrote appears to have been written with her grandchildren as the intended audience.

Following Britannia Kennon's death in January 1911, Armistead Jr. became the owner of Tudor Place. According to the terms of Britannia's will, her estate, including her possessions and the 5.5-acre Tudor Place property, was to be divided equally among her five grandchildren. The obvious solution to dividing the house and property evenly was to sell it and split the proceeds five ways. Fortunately, Armistead Jr. was able to buy out his siblings' shares and simultaneously forfeit his share of another family property, which allowed him to own Tudor Place outright. The siblings also devised a way to equally divide the family collection that had

been at Tudor Place since Thomas and Martha Peter purchased the property in 1805; it was no easy task, as this diverse collection included furniture, jewelry, clothing, and decorative objects formerly owned by George and Martha Washington as well as items associated with several generations of the Peter family. To ensure that the collection of Washington objects, and everything else at Tudor Place, was equally divided, Armistead Jr. and his siblings began the arduous task of inventorying more than a century's worth of family possessions. Each object was assigned a number and given a small sticker with that identifying number. Objects inherited by Martha Peter from her grandmother or those that she and Thomas Peter purchased at Mount Vernon at the 1802 sale received an additional paper "Mount Vernon" label. The siblings identified 529 items at Tudor Place that came from Mount Vernon, ranging from notable items such as Martha Washington's writing table to "a piece of soap of General and Mrs. Washington."[11] The 1911 inventory of Britannia Kennon's estate is an equally important historic document, describing each object and noting its location within the house. Armistead Jr. and his siblings Freeland and Agnes worked tirelessly to ensure that everything was split evenly and fairly among the three of them and their two other brothers. The process was conducted as follows: five numbers were placed into a bowl and each sibling drew a number. The siblings then commenced to choose objects, allowing the sibling who drew number one to select first and continuing in order until the one who drew number five made their selection. The process was repeated for more than thirty rounds until the collection was equally divided. One of the siblings, B. Kennon Peter, was unable to attend the division as he was living in Ohio at the time, so pieces were selected for him.

The nucleus of Tudor Place Historic House and Garden's Washington collection are the objects and papers that were selected by Armistead Jr. during the 1911 division of Britannia's estate. Some of the objects that left Tudor Place as part of the 1911 division of the estate have since returned to the museum collection, and others can now be found in the collections of Smithsonian's National Museum of American History, the Philadelphia Museum of Art, and, of course, Mount Vernon. Other pieces remain in private family collections still owned by Britannia's descendants.

The archive of family papers was also equally divided in 1911, although Armistead Jr. claimed that it was Britannia's intention for him to receive the bulk of the family archive and that his siblings were aware of her wishes.[12] However, as he later wrote, his siblings were adamant that the family papers, like the objects in the house, be equally divided among them. In that division, Armistead Jr. received his grandmother's account books, a portion of her correspondence, and many of the papers related to the 1844–45 settlement of the estate of her late husband, Capt. Beverley Kennon. Today the family archive that existed at Tudor Place until the time of Britannia Kennon's death is split among three institutional collections; the portion inherited by Armistead Jr. is now found in the Tudor Place Archive along with Mr. Peter's papers and those of generations of the Peter family who lived at Tudor Place. Other portions of the Peter family papers are found at the Fred W. Smith National Library for the Study of George Washington at Mount Vernon and in the Albert and Shirley Small Special Collections Library at the University of Virginia.

In addition to keeping his original notes transcribing the conversations with Britannia about the family's history, Armistead Jr. compiled a handwritten version where he anthologized a portion of the notes into a single document. At a later point, around 1920, he created a typescript version of the document as well. Each of these manuscript versions was consulted and considered to be a significant primary source for this editorial project. When discrepancies arose, such as the omission of sentences or the reordering of phrases in the later typescript version, the original notes from the "in person" conversations that Armistead Jr. had with Britannia were considered definitive and prioritized over the later versions. The later versions compiled by Armistead Jr. also include parenthetical asides that he made in order to provide contextual information about his grandmother or other family members she described. Examples include the reasons why Britannia, like her mother, always spoke of Martha Washington as "Grandmama Washington," and the exact dates of specific events such as the laying of the cornerstone of the US Capitol Building that Britannia's mother, Martha Custis Peter, attended and described to her many years later. Armistead Jr. also added clarification on names or dates of which Britannia was unclear or incorrect. All of these asides have been included in this version but are noted as being from Armistead Jr. so it is clear that they are later additions. In nearly all instances, Britannia's grandchildren were careful to note that they recorded what she said "verbatim" and recopied it as such.

In the two long-form versions of his grandmother's reminiscences that Armistead Jr. compiled, he added excerpts from late-nineteenth-century biographical works or compilations of letters and journals associated with people discussed in a particular passage, like George Ticknor or Gouverneur Morris. The locations of those excerpts are noted and fully cited, but the excerpts themselves have been omitted from this edition since they were not provided by Britannia. It is very plausible that Armistead Peter Jr. compiled many of his grandmother's reminiscences and added these references because he intended to publish the work, either as a book or as an article; but if that was his intention, it was never realized.

It is readily apparent to the reader that Britannia Kennon's Reminiscences as presented here are not necessarily in chronological order. Armistead Jr. and his siblings dated each section of conversational notes using the date on which Britannia recounted the information to them. The arrangement in this volume replicates the order in which Armistead Jr. compiled his grandmother's reminiscences, first in the handwritten version and later in the typescript compilation that he copied out at some point after Britannia's death. In addition to the information included in both of those versions, the final section of this edition includes further notes from conversations with Britannia that are found in Armistead Jr.'s papers but were omitted by him from the later long-form versions. His reasons for not including these fragments in his typescript version are unknown, but they are included herewith and arranged in chronological order as they contain important information about Tudor Place and the greater city

of Washington during the nineteenth century. Finally, several pages of undated notes found during this project are also included and presented in the order in which they are arranged in the folders of Armistead Jr.'s papers in the Tudor Place Archives.

From an editorial perspective, when discrepancies were observed, the original handwritten notes recorded in Britannia Kennon's presence or those passages written by her own hand "in compliance with a request from my grandson," served as the definitive source over the later typescripts and transcriptions.[13] The only corrections made to the original text when the various versions were transcribed for this edition were standardizations in the spelling of surnames. Many of the surviving notes written by the grandchildren make it clear that spelling of surnames such as Iturbide or Maltitz were written phonetically based on how Britannia pronounced them as she was recounting the information or sharing an anecdote. All other abbreviations and punctuation (or lack thereof) found in this volume faithfully reproduce what was found in the notes. Many of the notes survive only in an abbreviated form, and it is clear that certain words were omitted by the grandchildren in their haste to write down information as Britannia recounted it. In some instances, these missing words have been added but placed within brackets to clearly indicate that they are a later editorial addition and not part of the original document.

Given that many of these reminiscences were committed to paper in or after 1894, when Britannia Kennon was in her late eighties or early nineties, and that she was recalling events that had occurred sixty or seventy years earlier, her accuracy is impressive. In many instances, letters, receipts, or other papers found in the Peter family papers, both at Tudor Place and in other repositories, can corroborate the events and make it possible to precisely date an event Britannia described to her grandchildren, such as the funeral of her paternal grandmother Elizabeth Scott Peter or the amputation of an enslaved man's leg following a carriage accident.

When reading Britannia Kennon's Reminiscences, the reader must remember that she was recounting this information to her grandchildren. Thus, personal opinions are frequently included because her original audience was members of her close family. Always proper, Britannia undoubtedly would not have made some of the comments if her intended audience was more public. The reader should also understand that Britannia was a product of the time and place in which she grew up—the antebellum South—and that her family owned numerous enslaved individuals and used their labor in the Tudor Place household as well as on their agricultural lands in Maryland, where tobacco and other crops were raised.

An unapologetic Southerner, Britannia herself was a slave owner and grew up in relative comfort, due in part to her family's use of an enslaved labor force. Britannia's mother, Martha Parke Custis Peter, received two large bequests totaling more than one hundred "dower slaves" from the Custis estate. Thomas and Martha Peter gained ownership of the first group at the time of their 1795 marriage and received the second group after Martha Washington's death in 1802.[14] According to a seventeenth-century Virginia law, any children born to female dower slaves also became dower slaves regardless of the status of their father. In this way, the Peter family came to own multiple generations of dower slaves; many of these individuals were inherited by Britannia or her brother at the time of Martha Peter's death and remained in their ownership until the eventual abolition of slavery in the District of Columbia in 1862.

Following the February 28, 1844, death of her husband, Cdre. Beverley Kennon, Britannia hired out a number of the enslaved individuals that were previously used for the daily operation of their Washington household. In her role as the executrix of her husband's estate, Britannia also approved the sale of some sixty enslaved individuals from her late husband's Henrico County, Virginia, plantation. Her attitude toward slavery is apparent when she discusses several of the enslaved individuals at Tudor Place prior to the emancipation of slaves. In an aside about Hannah, the daughter of her enslaved lady's maid Barbara, Britannia recalled to her grandchildren that Hannah "belonged to me, of course."[15]

Britannia's attitude toward slavery was clearly one of matter-of-fact acceptance, as it was an institution that she had known and been surrounded by for the first five decades of her life. Her surviving letters as well as information she provided to her grandchildren suggest that, from her point of view, she was kind to the individuals she owned and she maintained relationships with her former slaves more than three decades after the abolition of slavery in the District of Columbia. Her account books include notations of charitable gifts to former slaves, and, in the very first passage of the reminiscences, she speaks again of Hannah and of the man who became her husband, Alfred Pope. Hannah and Alfred Pope both chose to remain in Georgetown following their 1850 emancipation, and Britannia described them to her grandchildren as "a most respected couple."[16]

One of the most intriguing relationships of Britannia's life was her role as employer to longtime Tudor Place gardener John Luckett, an escaped slave from Virginia whom she hired when slavery was still legal in the District of Columbia. Luckett remained in Britannia's employ at Tudor Place for more than forty-four years, until his death in 1906. In 1899 Luckett recounted the story of his escape from slavery to Armistead Jr., who later wrote about it in his own reminiscences.[17] While residing on a Fairfax County, Virginia, plantation in 1861–62, Luckett and several other enslaved men were seized by the Union Army as contraband. Not wanting to drive the army supply wagon that he was assigned to drive, Luckett escaped and crossed the Chain Bridge from Virginia into the District of Columbia. While walking down Congress (now 31st) Street in front of Tudor Place, he saw Britannia Kennon out in her garden and called out to her, inquiring if she needed to hire anyone.

It appears that their relationship evolved from employer and employee to friendship and mutual respect garnered by a lengthy association of more than four decades. Luckett was frequently called on by Britannia's grandchildren to take them fishing or hunting, and he attended important events in the lives of her grandchildren, including graduations and ordinations.[18] Upon hearing news of the birth of Armistead Jr.'s son in 1896,

Luckett asked Britannia to pass along the message that he felt "proud to hear that he has a son . . . and I hope I may live long enough to drag him around as I used to do [Armistead Jr.]"[19] Despite numerous offers by the Peter family to secure housing for Luckett and his family in closer proximity to Tudor Place, he always declined, stating that his wife preferred to reside in their neighborhood on Capitol Hill. At the time of Luckett's death in 1906, Britannia's granddaughter Agnes Peter wrote an obituary for the longtime gardener that appeared in Washington newspapers.[20] Britannia is quoted in the obituary, saying, "If I were asked to name a fault in John I could not do so. It is a pity there are not more like him."[21] In the late winter of 1911, when the contents of Tudor Place were inventoried after Britannia's death, the list of objects in her bedroom included a photograph of John Luckett—the only photograph in that room of someone who was not a member of the extended Custis-Peter family.[22]

For all the wealth of information that Britannia Kennon provides to her grandchildren in these reminiscences, she is relatively quiet about that transitional period in 1862–63 when enslaved labor was no longer used at Tudor Place and she began employing paid servants. In the District of Columbia, the emancipation of slavery occurred on April 16, 1862, when President Abraham Lincoln signed the District of Columbia Compensated Emancipation Act. This act provided for compensated emancipation, whereby slave owners who made an oath of loyalty to the Union and voluntarily emancipated their slaves would receive financial compensation, up to $300 for each individual they emancipated. This act was passed nearly nine months before President Lincoln signed the Emancipation Proclamation on January 1, 1863. It's not surprising that Britannia Kennon's name cannot be found in the surviving records of District slave owners who sought compensated emancipation, as it's doubtful that she would have been willing to sign a loyalty oath to the Union, given her overt Southern sympathies. As she describes in the reminiscences, she spent the first nine months of the Civil War traveling with her daughter, moving from one Southern town to another until she returned to Georgetown on January 1, 1862. It was later that spring that she decided to take in boarders, and the domestic staff hired at that time appear to be Irish immigrant servants—with the exception of Luckett as gardener.

Another tragic episode of her life that Britannia doesn't directly address in the conversations with her grandchildren is the death of her husband, Beverley Kennon, when she was just twenty-nine years old. Commodore Kennon was one of six victims killed when a deck gun exploded during a firing demonstration on board the USS *Princeton* on February 28, 1844. Britannia herself was on board the ship at the time of the tragedy, with the wives of other officers and politicians, but did not directly witness the explosion.

One can only imagine the loss that Britannia must have felt after just sixteen months of marriage; thus widowed, she was also a single parent to her infant daughter. Correspondence from other family members suggests that Britannia was devastated by the loss of her husband and spent nearly two weeks confined to her room.[23] It's plausible that the events surrounding the February 28, 1844, disaster on the *Princeton*

represented such a dark and painful time of her life that she couldn't bear to speak of it, even more than fifty years later. Another incident from February 1904 further illustrates the lasting effect that her husband's death and funeral had on her. That month Britannia received an invitation from President and Mrs. Theodore Roosevelt to attend an event at the White House. The invitation, now in the Tudor Place Archives, still retains the response card and other inserts, suggesting that Britannia did not return them or attend the event. While she was quite advanced in age by 1904 (she would have turned eighty-nine the previous month), it is likely that she had other reasons for not attending. The event to which she was invited was a reception to be held in the public rooms of the White House. It is very possible that Britannia associated these spaces, especially the East Room, with that very dark time in her life, as it was the location for the state funeral held for her husband and the Cabinet members killed aboard the *Princeton*.

When reading these recollections recorded by her grandchildren, it also becomes apparent that as Britannia advanced in age, she became someone unafraid to speak her mind. She recounted to her grandchildren that when the Reverend Dr. Jacob Asbury Regester, an Episcopal priest from Buffalo, New York, called on her at Tudor Place, she questioned his outspoken preference for northern seminaries after noting that he was an alumnus of the Virginia Theological Seminary in Alexandria, Virginia. Wanting to further her argument, she then named two other prominent New England bishops of the Episcopal Church—Henry Codman Potter, then bishop of New York, and

Britannia's aunt Eleanor "Nelly" Custis Lewis was a frequent visitor to Tudor Place. She lived at Woodlawn, adjacent to Mount Vernon. Portrait by John Beale Bordley. Image Courtesy of George Washington's Fredericksburg Foundation.

grand man now as he entered the door of the Parlor—his genial manner and dignified appearance making an impression on my mind which time cannot efface."[22] Among the gifts that Lafayette presented to Thomas and Martha Peter was an engraved portrait that has hung on the west wall of the Tudor Place drawing room for nearly two centuries.

Another result of Lafayette's visit to Tudor Place was the introduction of Britannia's sister America to her future husband, Lt. William G. Williams, an officer in the US Army's Topographical Corps. An 1824 graduate of the US Military Academy, Williams was an artist and surveyor as well as a friend of Britannia's brother George Washington Peter. Britannia later recalled that it was "Brother Washington" who invited a group of officers, including Williams, to attend the Tudor Place levee at which Lafayette was the guest of honor.[23] Williams's lineage is somewhat mysterious; he was given an appointment to West Point by Secretary of War John C. Calhoun of South Carolina when his family had no known connection to the Palmetto state. Williams's father, William Williams Sr., was English, and his mother was from Georgia. Both Lieutenant Williams and his sister were born in Philadelphia, and his parents later returned to England. Britannia's recollection of America's marriage to Lieutenant Williams omits any hints of the drama surrounding the event that is alluded to in surviving correspondence. Britannia was only eleven years old at the time, so she may not have realized that her parents were less than pleased with their now eldest daughter's intended husband. In the spring of 1826 Britannia's aunt Nelly Custis Lewis wrote to Lafayette's son Georges Lafayette in France

1824. The visit occurred during Lafayette's year-long national tour, which he made at the invitation of President James Monroe. During the 1824–25 tour, Lafayette visited the homes of all four of the Custis grandchildren in the District of Columbia and nearby Virginia. The general had previously met Britannia's mother when she was a young girl at Mount Vernon during his 1784 visit, so it was a joyful reunion. In the late nineteenth century Britannia told the story of the general's visit to a Washington newspaper reporter, saying, "I can see the describing her niece's future husband and his treatment of Thomas and Martha Peter. In the letter, she stated that Williams was "very obnoxious to her Parents. They are miserable, & entirely disapprove her choice but she is so entirely devoted to him, that all other ties appear weak in comparison with her love for one, who, 13 months since was a perfect stranger."[24] Even the wedding day was fraught with drama. America Peter had been unwell, and when Lieutenant Williams arrived at Tudor Place on the morning of June 27, 1826, to inquire about her health, she informed him that they were going to be married within the hour.[25] Rev. Walter Dulany Addison of St. John's Church, Georgetown, was summoned, and the couple was married in a brief ceremony that Ann Schaaff described as "like a funeral, all the family in tears and the bride almost in convulsions."[26]

A skilled artist who was later admitted to the National Academy of Design, Williams painted portraits of his fellow officers as well as of members of the Peter family, including his father-in-law, Thomas Peter. The composition of many of Williams's portraits, such as one in which his wife resembles the Madonna, evoke classical works that he observed while touring the museums of Europe. He completed a portrait of Britannia around 1830 in which he depicts her preparing to ascend a staircase in a cream-colored silk gown and holding her hat in hand.

Following her studies with the Misses Wrights, Britannia spent four years at the Young Ladies Academy at Georgetown's Visitation Convent. The girl's school in western Georgetown, established by the Sisters of the Order of the Visitation of Holy Mary, is still in operation more than two centuries later, known today as

The earliest image of Britannia is this portrait painted by her brother-in-law, William G. Williams, ca. 1828–30. Private collection.

Britannia spent four years as a pupil at the Young Ladies
Academy at Georgetown's Visitation Convent. Georgetown
Visitation campus buildings facing 35th Street.
Image courtesy Georgetown Visitation.

Britannia received this award as a Visitation student in 1828.
President of the United States John Quincy Adams presented
the awards during a ceremony at the end of the term.
Tudor Place Archives.

Georgetown Visitation Preparatory School. The school's academic program when Britannia attended was both intellectual and practical. In addition to mathematics, logic, English composition, and music, the curriculum included various domestic skills that would prepare the young ladies to manage a household and be accomplished wives and mothers.[27] Later in life, Britannia recalled that the Peter family's enslaved coachman, Will Johnson, "took me up before him on horseback & took me to the Convent in bad weather."

Examinations and exhibitions were held at the end of each school year, and premiums were distributed to students for their academic or artistic achievement. In 1828 President John Quincy Adams presided at the ceremony and awarded the premiums at the conclusion of the term. Three premiums awarded to Britannia during her four years at the academy survive, recognizing her achievements in needlework, music, and penmanship. More than seventy years later, Britannia recalled to her grandchildren that the only time she was ever punished while attending Visitation was for talking in class. As her punishment, the nun instructing the class ordered her to get down on her knees and kiss the floor of the classroom.[28] While the Young Ladies Academy was administered by Catholic nuns of the Visitation order, the institution was equally popular among both Catholic and Protestant families of Georgetown as well as the daughters of legislators, ambassadors, and even foreign dignitaries stationed in Washington. During Britannia's time at the school, her first cousin Henrietta Dunlop was also a pupil, as were four of the daughters of the deposed emperor of Mexico, Agustín de Iturbide.

Britannia spoke to her grandchildren of the Iturbide daughters on several occasions. Their father was a military leader who had a brief reign lasting for ten months in 1822–23 as Emperor Augustin I of Mexico, after which he abdicated and fled to Europe with his family. Upon returning to Mexico in the summer of 1824, the deposed emperor was captured and executed. His wife, the former Empress Anna María, and most of their children fled to the United States, residing first in New Orleans and eventually settling in Georgetown by 1826.[29] After living for a time at the convent, Madame Iturbide acquired a house on First Street (now N Street). Britannia recalled seeing the former empress in Georgetown, mentioning that she dressed as a nun during the period of time that she lived in the convent and spoke only in Spanish. Britannia also recalled that Madame Iturbide smoked tobacco in a small clay pipe.

During her time as a pupil at Visitation, Britannia met another woman who would become one of her lifelong friends, Ann Gertrude Wightt, then known as Sister Gertrude of the Visitation Order. Wightt was orphaned as a young girl after the deaths of both parents. She spent six years as a boarding student at the academy; then she took her vows in 1814. By the time Britannia was a pupil at the academy, Sister Gertrude was directress of the academy and assistant superior of the convent.[30] She held a number of administrative positions within the convent and the academy over the next two decades and enacted several reforms during her tenure as directress. After becoming disillusioned with convent life, Sister Gertrude left the convent in March of 1831 and never returned. While this is how Britannia recalled the events surrounding the nun's departure to her grandchildren, the actual reason for her flight is more political. Sister Gertrude was a reformer and, during her tenure as directress of the academy, she worked on several initiatives to improve the curriculum and enlarge the school. In 1831 she even attempted to change the order of the convent from the Visitation order to the Ursuline order.[31] When the attempt failed, she fled the convent. Wightt, whom Britannia said the pupils called "Sister Getty," was a cousin of nineteenth-century Washington socialite and philanthropist Marcia Burnes Van Ness, wife of Major General John Peter Van Ness. When Wightt made her initial escape in 1831 she first sought refuge at the Van Ness mansion, asking a coachman to take here there after she walked out of the convent.

In addition to the education Britannia received at Visitation, she was also given instruction in music and dance, two skills of refinement considered necessary for a young woman of her class during the nineteenth century. Helen Simpson of Georgetown was Britannia's music teacher and oversaw her instruction on the piano.[32] For her dancing class, instructor Pierre Landrin Duport came to Tudor Place and taught Britannia and several other young ladies of the neighborhood, including Mildred Lee, a sister of Robert E. Lee; Henrietta Dunlop, Britannia's cousin; and Anna Maria Calhoun, the daughter of Vice President John C. Calhoun.[33] Duport was a French émigré who claimed to have taught the children of Marie Antoinette prior to fleeing France during the revolution. After first settling in Philadelphia in 1790 he made his way to Washington, DC. Surviving receipts for Britannia's lessons suggest that Duport charged ten dollars per quarter per pupil.

In February 1830 Britannia's eldest brother, John Parke Custis Peter, married Elizabeth Jane Henderson in Montgomery County, Maryland. Britannia, her aunt Arianna Calvert, and her cousin Robert Dunlop made the ten-mile journey from Georgetown to Montanverd, her uncle George Peter's estate, on the morning of the wedding. The following evening, February 5, Thomas and Martha Peter held a ball at Tudor Place to celebrate their eldest son's marriage.[34] By that summer Tudor Place was a multigenerational household as several of Thomas and Martha Peter's grown children and their offspring were now residing in the house, in addition to the now-fifteen-year-old Britannia. Newlyweds John and Elizabeth were living at Tudor Place, and she was expecting their first child, who would be born there the following winter.[35] Daughter America and two of her children also returned to Tudor Place in June 1830 when her husband, Lieutenant Williams, sailed for Europe, where he would spend the next year seeking additional artistic training and visiting his parents in England. That spring and summer Britannia frequently joined her mother and older sister in making social calls around Georgetown and Washington to members of their extended family and other ladies, including the now-widowed Anna Maria Thornton. Mrs. Thornton's diary entry of April 30, 1831 notes, "Mrs. Peter, [America Peter] Williams, and Britannia called."[36]

In addition to her immediate family at Tudor Place, many members of the extended Custis and Peter families also lived in Georgetown, in nearby southern Maryland, or just across the Potomac River in Virginia. Britannia frequently spent time with her

Dunlop cousins, the children of her aunt Elizabeth Peter Dunlop. The Dunlops, like the Peters, split their year between Georgetown and Hayes, their estate in Montgomery County, Maryland. Britannia's cousin Robert Dick as well as her cousins Jane and Elizabeth Peter also lived in Georgetown and were very close to her in age. Similarly, her cousin Angela Lewis of Woodlawn was the youngest daughter of Nelly Custis Lewis and was just two years older than Britannia. Finally, Mary Anna Custis, the only daughter of George Washington Parke Custis, resided at Arlington House, which Britannia recalled visiting on numerous occasions, journeying there by taking the ferry across the Potomac. When Mary wed an army officer named Robert E. Lee in the Arlington House parlor on June 30, 1831, Britannia was a member of the wedding party. For the rest of her life, she would always refer to General Lee as "Cousin Robert." In her reminiscences, Britannia recounted a rather humorous episode from the Lee wedding concerning Rev. Reuel Keith, the clergyman who performed the ceremony. On the day of the wedding Keith was traveling by buggy from Alexandria, where he served as the president of the Virginia Theological Seminary. Somewhere on the road between Alexandria and the Arlington estate, Reverend Keith was caught in a summer thunderstorm and thoroughly drenched. Upon arriving at Arlington House, the tall and lanky minister was given a pair of dry trousers belonging to Britannia's uncle Custis, who was noticeably shorter and stouter. According to Britannia, the inseam of the borrowed trousers was somewhat shorter than the reverend's own, resulting in a visible gap of several inches from the bottom of the

pant leg to the top of his boot. This made enough of an impression that Britannia fondly recalled it to her grandchildren more than sixty years later.[37]

Britannia was only nineteen years old when her father, Thomas Peter, died at Tudor Place in the spring of 1834 following a short illness. Much later in life, she recalled to her grandchildren how one of their favorite pastimes as father and daughter was to take long horseback rides over the family's land.[38] According to the terms of Thomas Peter's will, his sons, John Parke Custis Peter and George Washington Peter, each received one-third of his estate, while Britannia and her older sister, America, each received a half share of the final third. Britannia's mother, Martha, assumed management of the family's business interests and agricultural holdings in the district and Montgomery County, Maryland. She would remain in that role for the next twenty years until her death.

In February of 1840 Britannia's brother George Washington Peter married Jane Boyce, the daughter of a Georgetown neighbor, Capt. William Boyce. The Boyce family lived at Montrose, a large estate on Road Street adjacent to Tudor Place. For unknown reasons, Martha Peter didn't approve of her son's choice of a bride, so, as Britannia recounted to her grandson many years later, no members of the Peter family attended the wedding.[39]

Britannia herself wouldn't marry until late in 1842, a month before her twenty-eighth birthday. A letter written by Britannia's aunt Mary Custis suggests that sometime around 1838 Britannia fell in love with and hoped to marry a Georgetown newspaper editor named John L. O'Sullivan. The letter indicates that while Britannia was enamored with O'Sullivan, Martha Custis Peter opposed the match for her youngest daughter on the grounds that the young man was "without property of any kind and has hitherto not been successful in the application of his talents to produce a permanent result."[40] Two years later, in November of 1841, a forty-eight-year-old widower US Navy captain named Beverley Kennon had made a social call at Tudor Place.[41] He was accompanied by his distant cousin, Maria Beverley Clarke, the widowed daughter of Robert Beverley who resided at Acrolophos, directly across Road Street from Tudor Place. Also a descendant of the prominent Beverley family of Virginia, Kennon was serving as commandant of the Washington Navy Yard at the time of the visit.[42] A career naval officer, he was a veteran of the Second Barbary War and the War of 1812. Kennon's father, Richard Kennon, had served with distinction on General Washington's staff during the American Revolution and later accepted an appointment by President Thomas Jefferson to be the first governor of the Louisiana Territory.[43] The purpose of the call at Tudor Place was likely for Captain Kennon to be introduced to Britannia. However, Britannia wasn't at home that November day. Several weeks later, they were formally introduced at the Octagon House, where both were attending a reception held to celebrate the recent marriage of Col. John Tayloe's daughter Ann Ogle Tayloe. Kennon had been a widower for nine years and was likely looking to remarry. His first wife, Elizabeth Claiborne Kennon, had died in 1832, just five days after the birth of their second son.

In the spring of 1842 Britannia and her mother learned that America Peter Williams, now living in Buffalo, New York, was gravely ill. In 1838 America and her children had traveled north to Buffalo to join her husband, now a captain in the US Army's Topographical Engineers. While in Buffalo, Captain Williams was engaged in surveys for improving the city's harbor on Lake Erie. In those intervening years, America had given birth to several additional children, only one of whom survived. She had also accompanied her husband when his surveying work took him to Detroit in the newly created state of Michigan and to Green Bay and Milwaukee in the Wisconsin Territory before they returned to Buffalo in late 1841. Martha Peter first received word of America's illness when a letter arrived at Tudor Place on April 27.[44] Unknown to her at the time, America had actually died two days prior, on April 25, 1842, at age thirty-eight. Word of America's death reached Tudor Place several days later, on April 29. "I heard last evening that America Williams is no more," Anna Maria Thornton recorded in her diary.[45] America had written to her mother only a few weeks before, stating that she planned to bring her children to Georgetown for a lengthy visit later that summer. The day after the news of America's death reached Georgetown, Mrs. Thornton called and found Martha Peter and Britannia "much afflicted, but more composed than I feared."[46] Although she never directly commented on it to her grandchildren, or in any other surviving writings, Britannia was clearly affected by the loss of her older sister. While a difference of twelve years separated the two sisters, Britannia was especially close to America, whom she called "Meck." Both were confirmed at the same time at St. John's Church on Lafayette Square. The Peter family didn't normally attend this church, but the sisters were confirmed there because Rev. John Thomson Brooke, the rector of the church they attended, Georgetown's Christ Church, refused to confirm anyone who did not renounce dancing.[47] Soon after America's death, Britannia stepped in to help her mother raise America's five children, including nephew Orton, who was not yet four years old at the time of his mother's death. America's widowed husband felt that he couldn't care for their children while he was constantly traveling, so they were sent to live at Tudor Place. The Williams children were truly orphaned four years later, in September 1846, when Captain Williams was killed while leading a charge during the Battle of Monterrey.

In the meantime, Kennon's courtship of Britannia continued, and she accepted his proposal of marriage. On December 6, 1842, Commodore Kennon wrote to the Reverend John Hoff of Georgetown's Christ Church requesting that he be present at Tudor Place "on the evening of the 8th instant, to marry me."[48] Britannia wed Beverley Kennon in the Tudor Place drawing room on the evening of December 8, 1842. According to diarist Anna Maria Thornton, "it rained all day and poured in the evening," which prevented her from attending the nuptials.[49] Britannia's attendants were friends and family members, including her first cousins Henrietta and Elizabeth Dunlop as well as her niece Martha "Markie" Williams. The cream-colored silk gown Britannia wore for the ceremony still survives in the Tudor Place collection.

Following the marriage, Britannia moved into Kennon's residence, the Commandant's House also known as Quarters A, at the Washington Navy Yard.

From this house, centrally located on the crest of a hill just east of the Navy Yard's Main Gate, Britannia would have had a "sweeping view of the workshops and laborers in the gently sloping vista below the house."[50] In addition to Kennon's two sons, several members of his extended family, including two sisters-in-law and a nephew, lived in the house. When she moved to the Navy Yard, Britannia brought her enslaved lady's maid, Barbara, as well as Hannah, who was Barbara's teen-aged daughter, and Charles, an enslaved groom and coachman. The move across the city would have been an adjustment for Britannia, who was accustomed to the bucolic, tree-lined streets of upper Georgetown. Located in the southeastern portion of the District of Columbia on a deep-water channel of the Anacostia River, then called the Eastern Branch of the Potomac River, the Washington Navy Yard was established in 1799 and was the largest shipbuilding facility in the United States for several decades of the nineteenth century.[51] The city's commercial wharves and warehouses were located in the neighborhoods surrounding the Navy Yard, so it would have been a noisy and odorous place in 1842. The river adjacent to the Naval Yard was frequently used as a sewer, resulting in contaminated drinking water and the threat of diseases such as cholera and typhus.[52] Another danger was the risk of explosions. The Navy Yard housed the laboratories where highly explosive artillery shells and experimental types of ordnance were developed and tested. During Commodore Kennon's twenty-three-month tenure as commandant, two explosions occurred that resulted in the deaths of workers or sailors. The first incident, on September 7, 1841, in the armorers' shop, was the result of a shell prematurely exploding, killing one worker. A second explosion, on June 27, 1842, occurred in the laboratory after two shells burst in rapid succession, killing two workers and severely injuring others.[53] However, both disasters occurred before Britannia's move to the Navy Yard.

In March of 1843 Beverley Kennon was promoted to chief of the navy's Bureau of Construction and Repair. As part of the reorganization of the navy in 1842, Secretary Abel P. Upshur recommended abolishing the three-person Board of Naval Commissioners, which had served as the main administrative body since 1815, and transferring its powers and duties to five bureaus. Each bureau was headed by a chief officer whose appointment was made by the President of the United States with the approval of the Senate.[54] The Kennons soon purchased a house and lot on H Street, near the President's House and the adjacent Navy Department Building. The move would allow Kennon to live in closer proximity to his office and allow the incoming commandant, Capt. John H. Aulick, to occupy the Commandant's House in the Navy Yard.[55] The move also placed Britannia in much closer proximity to the growing commercial and retail district along Pennsylvania Avenue where numerous shops were located. By the time the Kennons purchased their H Street house, Britannia was several months pregnant. Their only child, a daughter whom they named Martha Custis Kennon and called "Markie," was born at Tudor Place on October 18, 1843. Britannia seems to have purposely journeyed back to Tudor Place for her accouchement and remained with her mother for at least a month afterward.[56] As Anna Maria Thornton had

done for Britannia's birth nearly thirty years earlier, she recorded Markie's birth in her diary, noting, "Britannia Kennon (late Peter) had a daughter."[57] In addition to motherhood, Britannia now had her own household to manage in downtown Washington. However, her married life would last for only sixteen months.

On the morning of February 28, 1844, Britannia, Commodore Kennon, and her niece Martha Williams were among a party of four hundred guests who sailed down the Potomac on board the USS *Princeton*, one of the US Navy's newest warships. Laid down at Philadelphia's Navy Yard, the *Princeton* was a fully rigged vessel that also featured steam propulsion and a screw propeller. It had been launched five months earlier, in September 1843, the brainchild of engineer John Ericsson and Capt. Robert Stockton. As the head of the US Navy's Bureau of Construction as well as the former commandant of the Washington Navy Yard, Kennon was an important ally for President John Tyler to have on board the ship that day. Tyler had plans to expand the US Navy, which required congressional approval and a sizable appropriation, so he used the ship and its two impressive deck guns, the Peacemaker and the Oregon, as part of his justification for the expansion. Members of Congress and other dignitaries were invited to tour the ship and see a demonstration of its firepower. Britannia and Martha set out from the H Street house in a carriage that morning with little idea of the tragedy that would befall the family later that day. After stopping to pick up Commodore Kennon around eleven o'clock, they boarded a small steamer at the Washington Steamboat Wharf, which took them downriver to Alexandria where the USS *Princeton* was

Martha Parke Custis Peter with
her granddaughter, Martha "Markie"
Custis Kennon, ca. 1850. Mrs. Peter
is holding the portrait miniature of
President George Washington
that she received in 1795.
Tudor Place Archives.

docked.[58] The ship "presented a most magnificent appearance, being completely manned, and Decorated with the flags of the different nations," Martha wrote that day in her diary.[59] It was a very social atmosphere on board the ship, with food and musical entertainment. President Tyler as well as his secretary of state, Abel Parker Upshur, and secretary of the navy, Thomas Walker Gilmer, were present. Senators Thomas Hart Benton of Missouri and Levi Woodbury of New Hampshire were also on board, as was former first lady Dolley Madison.

The boat set off, heading south from Alexandria. The largest deck gun, the Peacemaker, was fired several times, its recoil shaking the entire vessel. It was Navy Secretary Gilmer who urged Captain Stockton to fire the gun a third time, just as the boat was passing Fort Washington on the Maryland shore, as they steamed back upriver. By this time, most of the guests had gone below decks to enjoy the luncheon set out for them while Commodore Kennon stayed to watch the firing of the gun. Britannia's niece Markie was seated "on a little bench around the helm of the boat" and watched as the crew prepared to once again fire the Peacemaker.[60]

As Captain Stockton pulled the firing lanyard, the large gun exploded, sending metal shrapnel across the deck and through the crowd of those standing nearby. Commodore Kennon was killed instantly along with Gilmer and Upshur. There were six victims in all, including President Tyler's enslaved valet Armistead. The deck was strewn with severed limbs and wounded bystanders. Twenty onlookers, including Senator Benton

AWFUL EXPLOSION OF THE "PEACE-MAKER" ON BOARD THE U.S. STEAM FRIGATE, PRINCETON, ON WEDNESDAY, 28.TH FEB.T 1844.

Britannia's husband, Beverley Kennon, was killed in an explosion on board
the USS *Princeton* on February 28, 1844, depicted in this engraving by Currier & Ives.
Library of Congress.

of Missouri and Captain Stockton, were injured by the blast but ultimately survived. Lt. R. E. Thompson later wrote in the *Princeton*'s log that the Peacemaker broke off at the trunnion band and breech and split in half.[61] A Naval Board of Inquiry was convened and later absolved Stockton of any blame for the disaster. The Committee of Science and Arts of Philadelphia's Franklin Institute further investigated the explosion, ultimately determining that it resulted from the use of wrought iron rather than cast iron in the construction of the gun.[62]

Initially, Britannia was told that her husband was merely wounded, not killed, and that she should go home and prepare his room. Family members who knew the truth concealed it from her until she could be taken home. It was there in her house on H Street that her older brother George Washington Peter broke the news to her of Commodore Kennon's death. "The effect on her was most distressing," her niece Martha Williams noted. Britannia "kept to her bed for several days & her grief was almost too much to bear." Through her fog of grief, she also wanted to be told exactly what happened, insisting "on knowing all the particulars & Washington told her everything."[63] Several days after the accident, President Tyler wrote to Britannia offering his condolences, stating, "You have lost a kind and devoted husband and I have lost a warm and devoted friend."[64]

After the disaster, the *Princeton* steamed to the Washington Navy Yard. The *National Intelligencer* newspaper noted that the bodies of the victims, including Captain Kennon, were left on the ship until the following day, when they were placed in caskets and taken to the President's House for a state funeral.[65] Once there, the caskets were placed in the East Room, and glass viewing plates in each casket allowed the mourners to see each of the victims at rest. Captain Kennon's face had to be covered with a white cloth because of disfigurement caused by the explosion. Rev. Clement Moore Butler of St. John's Episcopal Church in Georgetown delivered the funeral sermon that day at the President's House. Britannia kept a copy of this sermon, later printed as a pamphlet, which is now found among her papers in the Tudor Place Archives.

In a letter to former president Andrew Jackson, Francis P. Blair described the funeral: "The last year of this Administration is entered upon with a carnage of the cabinet, which has made the East room look like a charnel House. The bodies of five friends of the president have just been borne out of his mansion. The day is suitable to the sad scene. The Heavens are hung with black."[66]

Following the ceremony, President Tyler personally led the procession of mourners down Pennsylvania Avenue to Congressional Cemetery, where Commodore Kennon and the other victims were laid to rest. The bodies were temporarily placed in the public vault until the graves could be prepared. With the assistance of her brother-in-law, Dr. George Kennon, Britannia purchased a grave for her husband, who was buried adjacent to several of the other victims, a single obelisk marking their graves.[67] Now a twenty-nine-year-old widow with a four-month-old infant, Britannia leased the H Street house and returned to Tudor Place to live with her mother. "Mrs. Kennon has gone to her mother's in Geo. Town," Annie Payne, the niece of former first lady Dolley Madison, noted in a March 22, 1844, letter.[68]

Cdre. Beverley Kennon had this daguerreotype taken at the Washington studio of Matthew Brady in 1844 just a few weeks before his death. 1899 photo of an 1844 daguerreotype, Tudor Place Archives.

Just a month before his death Beverley Kennon had drafted a new will, likely to ensure that his infant daughter "Markie" would inherit a share of his estate. The will also named Britannia as executrix of his estate and entitled her to the H Street house, which he noted was purchased with her money, as well as the property she had inherited from her father's estate ten years earlier.[69] In her role as executrix of her late husband's estate, Britannia was not only responsible for the settlement of his affairs in the District of Columbia but also for Solitaire, his eight-hundred-acre plantation in Henrico County, Virginia. Working with her late husband's cousin as her attorney in Virginia, Britannia approved the sale of a portion of the Virginia land not inherited by her stepsons as well as fifty enslaved individuals associated with the property. The commissioner's sale took place on December 20, 1844. Immediately after the commissioners' sale, a "Sale of Negroes" took place for, according to the advertisement, "50 likely negroes, part of which belong to the estate of Beverley Kennon, the remainder to George Kennon, Britannia W. Kennon, Executrix."[70] Notes found in Britannia's papers in the Tudor Place Archives suggest that the slaves belonging to Commodore Kennon's estate were sold for $4,238, compared to the personal property, which sold for only $976.[71] Several enslaved individuals from the Kennons' DC household were sold in Washington, while others were retained by Britannia and accompanied her back to Tudor Place.

Britannia's daughter, Martha "Markie" Kennon, was christened at St. John's Episcopal Church in Georgetown on March 28, 1844, the one-month anniversary of Commodore Kennon's death. "On the 28th

March, being the day one month on which its poor father was killed, Aunt Brit wished to have it christen'd," Britannia's niece Martha Williams noted in a letter describing her cousin's baptism.[72] Williams also mentions the occasion in her diary, commenting, "Aunt Brit's baby was christened today by Mr. Butler."[73] Around her infant daughter's neck, Britannia placed a heart-shaped locket containing plated strands of Commodore Kennon's hair. The locket was a gift that Kennon had given his infant daughter the month before his death.[74]

By the fall of 1844, Britannia, her daughter Markie, and her widowed mother Martha Custis Peter as well as four of her nieces and nephews—the children of her sister America Peter Williams—composed the Tudor Place household. In addition to helping raise these orphaned nieces and nephews, Britannia played an active role in the lives of her stepsons, Beverley Kennon Jr. and William Dandridge Kennon. The boys were enrolled in school in Richmond, Virginia, but Britannia's account books suggest that she visited them frequently and provided funds for their clothing and education.[75] Britannia also leased the H Street house, receiving monthly rent from a variety of tenants, including Elizabeth Schuyler Hamilton, the aged widow of Alexander Hamilton. Mrs. Hamilton had come to Washington in 1848 to live with her widowed daughter Eliza Hamilton Holly while she petitioned the government to purchase her husband's papers from his tenure as the first secretary of the treasury. Britannia recalled that Mrs. Hamilton and her daughter were good tenants, "paying the rent always on the day it was due."[76] Eliza Hamilton died in Britannia's H Street house on November 9, 1854.[77] In the year prior to her death, Mrs.

After her husband's death, Britannia remained close to both of her stepsons. She is pictured here with William Dandridge "Dan" Kennon, ca. 1845. Private collection, photograph by Peter Waddell.

Britannia Kennon with her daughter, Martha,
whom she called "Markie," ca. 1846.
Tudor Place Archives.

Hamilton sent Britannia a knitted pillow cover, which is still in the Tudor Place collection. Britannia carefully affixed a note identifying it as a piece made by Mrs. Hamilton and attached a clipped signature from one of Mrs. Hamilton's letters.

When the census taker visited Tudor Place on July 10, 1850, for the enumeration of the US federal census, he noted that there were six women living in the house: the head of the household was Britannia's seventy-three-year-old widowed mother, Martha Custis Peter. Residing with her was Britannia, then thirty-five; Britannia's five-year-old daughter, Markie; and three nieces: Martha "Markie" Williams, Columbia "Lum" Williams, and Kate Alicia Williams. By this time both Columbia and Kate Williams were enrolled as pupils at Miss Lydia English's Seminary in Georgetown.

By the summer of 1854 Martha Custis Peter's health was failing. When Anna Maria Thornton called at Tudor Place on July 10, she found a number of concerned family members present, including Martha's brother George Washington Parke Custis and his daughter Mary Anna Custis Lee as well as Mrs. Peter's daughter-in-law Jane. Martha Custis Peter died in the early hours of July 13, 1854.[78] As her great-niece Agnes Lee noted in her diary, "Aunt Peter died on the 13th July 1854 about two A.M. She was buried at Oaklands the home of one of her sons. She had heart disease but it was principally old age. She was more than seventy five. She led a very active wearing life working hard from preference giving herself no indulgences, but it was long before her strong constitution gave way. She lay dying for three days O what agony for her children."[79]

According to the terms of her mother's will, Britannia inherited the Tudor Place property. By this time, Britannia and her elder brother George Washington Peter were the only surviving heirs. "Washington," as he was called, already had property in Maryland that he had inherited from their father's estate. In contrast, Britannia's future was uncertain. A widow with a young daughter, her only source of income in addition to the bequest outlined in Commodore Kennon's will was a monthly widow's pension of fifty dollars that she received from the Department of the Navy. By inheriting the Tudor Place property, Britannia would always have a house and would not be reliant on finding another husband who could provide the necessary property and financial security. Martha Peter's will also included instructions for Britannia to sell off the northernmost portion of the Tudor Place property and for the proceeds from the sale to be used for the support of her orphaned granddaughters: Martha "Markie" Williams, Columbia "Lum" Williams, and Kate Alicia Williams. In accordance with her mother's wishes, Britannia sold the northernmost 1.5 acres of the property bounding Road (now R) Street. In addition to reducing the size of the property from its original 8.5 acres, another consequence of the sale was the loss of the entrance drive from R Street, so a new entrance and carriage drive was created on the eastern side of the property entering off Congress (now 31st) Street.

As Martha Peter had advanced in age, Britannia began to take over much of the day-to-day operation of Tudor Place. This included some needed maintenance and repairs. When Mrs. Thornton visited Tudor Place

Martha "Markie" Custis Williams was one of Britannia's nieces who came to live at Tudor Place in 1842 following the death of her mother. Her surviving diaries and letters provide important details about Britannia's life and Tudor Place. Tudor Place Archives.

on November 25, 1853, she later noted in her diary, "Went to Mrs. Peter's did not stay as she is painting and in confusion."[80] The painting might have been related to several interior improvements that were undertaken at that time and continued into the first few years of Britannia's ownership of the property. One such improvement was the addition of a central heating system that fed hot air from a cellar furnace through ductwork and out into rooms via brass and soapstone floor and wall grates. During the first few years of Britannia's ownership, Tudor Place was also piped for gas lighting.[81]

Several months after Martha Peter's death, Ann Gertrude Wightt, the former "Sister Gertrude" of Visitation Convent, came back to Georgetown and was invited by Britannia to join the Tudor Place household. By this time, both Wightt's cousin Marcia Burnes Van Ness and her husband, Major General Van Ness, with whom Wightt previously lived, were deceased. "She always said that she loved me better than anyone in the world," Britannia later recalled to her grandchildren of Wightt.[82] Only sixteen years older, "Sister Getty" was like an older sister to Britannia, whose own sisters, Columbia and America, were now deceased. Wightt was also like an aunt to Britannia's now eleven-year-old daughter, Markie, who even called her "Aunt Wightt" in surviving correspondence.[83] The former nun became a regular presence at Tudor Place and around Georgetown. When Anna Maria Thornton visited Tudor Place on November 10, 1854, she noted in her diary that Wightt was also there.[84] When Augusta Blanche Berard visited Tudor Place with Mary Custis Lee and Markie Williams in 1856, Britannia was away,

but they found "Miss Wight, the escaped Nun I once told you of. She is living with Mrs. K[ennon]." Berard went on to note that Wightt was "a very accomplished & agreeable person & extremely kind."[85] Wightt even appears with members of the Peter family on the membership list of Georgetown's Christ Church.[86]

The deaths of her husband, both parents, and two of her siblings within a ten-year period clearly took a toll on Britannia. In that same 1856 letter, Berard described seeing Britannia, now forty-one years old, for the first time in several years, remarking, "she is so changed. What has become of the proud tall Miss Britannia Peter of whom as a child I stood in such awe, I am sure I don't know."[87]

Once Markie became old enough, Britannia enrolled her at William J. Clarke's Georgetown Female Seminary, just a few blocks from Tudor Place. Clarke had taken over the school previously known as Miss English's Seminary (where Columbia and Kate Williams attended) after its namesake's retirement in 1852. Next Markie was sent to the Ingleside School for Girls near Catonsville, Maryland, and in 1858 she was enrolled in The Misses Casey's Young Ladies Day & Boarding School in Philadelphia. Britannia clearly wanted Markie to have the opportunity she was never afforded but was enjoyed by her sisters—an education in Philadelphia. Surviving correspondence between mother and daughter from this time period and from a later time when Markie frequently stayed with her uncle George Washington Peter and his family in Howard County, Maryland, is filled with information about goings on at Tudor Place. Another family member frequently mentioned in these letters is Britannia's stepson Bev, who by this time was the sailing master on a series of US Navy vessels. During his past decade of naval service, Bev had visited such exotic lands as China, the Hawaiian Islands, and French Polynesia, and he frequently wrote to both Britannia and Markie, informing them of his travels and adventures in these far corners of the world.[88]

The diary of Elizabeth Lindsay Lomax of Washington provides additional clues about this period in Britannia Kennon's life. Mrs. Lomax, the widow of Maj. Mann Page Lomax, was living in Washington and was a frequent guest at Tudor Place, while Britannia was a familiar guest to tea at Mrs. Lomax's house. Lomax noted on April 1, 1857, "We are dining with Mrs. Kennon at Tudor Place on Saturday evening." On May 7, 1857, she wrote, "Mrs. Kennon wishes us to dine with her again at Tudor Place next Tuesday evening. I love to go there. Tudor Place is delightfully situated on the Heights of Georgetown with a beautiful view of the Potomac and hills of Virginia."[89]

By 1858 Britannia was living alone at Tudor Place. Her daughter, Markie, was away at boarding school, and all of Britannia's nieces and nephews had reached adulthood and moved away. Eyeing potential revenue from renting the large house and property, Britannia leased Tudor Place to the family of attorney William Armistead Pendleton and rented rooms for herself in the home of another Georgetown widow, Mrs. Abbott, on nearby P Street. Surviving newspaper ads suggest that Britannia had tried to rent Tudor Place as early as 1856, but no tenant was found until 1858.[90] Britannia and Markie, now a young woman of seventeen, were planning to travel north in the spring of 1861 to accompany

Prior to the outbreak of the Civil War, Britannia's daughter Martha "Markie" Custis Kennon, seen here ca. 1860, attended boarding school in Philadelphia. Tudor Place Archives.

In 1840, artist James Glass drew this sketch, which he titled,
A Party in Georgetown at Mrs. Peter's Tudor Place. Collection of
Tudor Place Historic House & Garden.

the Casey sisters to the White Mountains in New Hampshire, but the outbreak of the Civil War altered their plans. As a slave-owning Southerner, Britannia was sympathetic to the Confederate cause and even assisted her cousin Mary Lee by sending wagons to Arlington House to transport the Lees' furniture and possessions, many of which were stored in the Tudor Place attic for the duration of the war.[91]

Rather than travel north, Britannia and Markie headed southwest from the District of Columbia into Virginia's Shenandoah Valley, where they settled in the town of Staunton. Living with Mrs. Lomax, who was also in Staunton, they remained until July of 1861. While there, Markie attended a ball at the American Hotel on June 13, keeping and pressing the flowers she received that evening.[92] Confederate general Robert S. Garett's defeat at the Battle of Cheat Mountain, just seventy-five miles west of the town, made Staunton vulnerable to Union attack, so Britannia and Markie left the Shenandoah Valley and traveled east to Richmond, Virginia. At the time Richmond was the capitol of the Confederacy and the location of the Confederate government. Shortly after their arrival in Richmond, Britannia encountered her cousin Gen. Robert E. Lee as she was walking down the street. More than thirty years later, she recalled their conversation to her grandchildren: "Well, Cousin Brit, what brought you down here?" the general asked her. "To put myself under your protection!" she replied.[93] In Richmond, the refugees stayed for four months in a boarding house run by Mrs. Dabney that was located at the corner of Franklin Street and 3rd Street. When finances became an issue in November 1861, they moved further south to

Petersburg, remaining for a month at another boarding house run by a Mrs. Page. This nomadic existence was common for many genteel Southern women during the Civil War.[94]

While Britannia was in Petersburg, she learned that the Union Army had begun to seize buildings around Georgetown, including private homes, for use as hospitals and headquarters buildings. She became fearful that Tudor Place, now empty after the departure of her tenants, would also be confiscated. She began making arrangements to return to Georgetown. Adding to her anxiety was the knowledge that the Seminary Building, the school located just a few blocks from Tudor Place, had already been seized for use as an officer's hospital by the Union Army. This was the building where Britannia had secured space to place her household furniture, including many pieces formerly owned by George and Martha Washington, during the time she leased Tudor Place. At Britannia's request, her cousin Robert Dick and a family friend, Dr. Joshua Riley, got wagons and hauled her furnishings from the Seminary Building to another building on Bridge Street where these objects could be safely stored for the duration of the war.

After leaving Petersburg in late November 1861, Britannia and Markie traveled east to Norfolk, Virginia, where they stayed for several days with Terry Sinclair, a Confederate naval officer who was also a nephew of Britannia's late husband. Sinclair was a member of the wedding party when Britannia and Commodore Kennon were married in 1842 and was the third generation of his family to serve as an officer in the US Navy prior to resigning his commission to join the Confederate Navy at the onset of the Civil War. At Britannia's insistence, he made inquiries to Gen. Benjamin Huger, the Confederate commander of the Department of Norfolk and the officer responsible for the defense of coastal Virginia. With Huger's approval, Britannia and Markie departed Norfolk on board a Confederate boat on December 5, 1861.[95] In the middle of Hampton Roads, they were transferred to a "flag of truce" vessel and taken to Fort Monroe, the Union-held fort located on Old Point Comfort. As Southerners, Britannia and Markie were required to remain on board the boat while the rest of the passengers debarked at the fort. Reporters came on board and tried to get news from the ladies but failed. That night at Fort Monroe an officer came aboard and told Britannia that he was obliged to search their baggage: "I told him he was welcome to search our trunks and handed him the keys," she later recalled.[96] After their trunks were searched, they were allowed to sail north the following day to Baltimore. From Baltimore they traveled west to Lynwood, the estate of Britannia's brother George Washington Peter located near Ellicott Mills, Maryland. After remaining there for a week, Britannia departed for Tudor Place, leaving Markie safely in the care of her uncle and aunt.

Arriving back at Tudor Place on January 1, 1862, Britannia found the house empty. The Pendletons, her tenants, were also Southern sympathizers and had fled further south to Richmond. Later that spring, as a further measure to prevent the seizure of the house, Britannia began taking in boarders who were Union Army officers or doctors associated with the military hospitals in Georgetown. Britannia and Markie even relocated to rooms on the second floor of the east wing, freeing up the larger bedchambers for paying tenants.

Britannia later recounted that she had people from nearly every state in the Union, and nearly all of them were Yankees. As she told her grandchildren thirty years later, the one rule she enforced among her tenants was that the war not be discussed during mealtimes since they were aware of her pro-Southern sentiments and she was aware of theirs as Northerners.[97]

To Britannia, it must have felt as if she was living in an army camp. In addition to the officers living under her own roof, like generals David Hunter and Lewis Addison Grant, a house a short distance away was leased by Gen. Henry W. Halleck, the general-in-chief of the Union Army. Just to the rear of that R Street property was a barracks that housed a detail of Union soldiers. The bugle reveilles and noise from this camp could have easily been heard from Tudor Place and must have been a constant reminder of the Union Army's presence in Georgetown. Britannia recalled that one day during the time she had the Union officers as boarders, her brother George Washington Peter and their cousin Barbara Dunlop were at Tudor Place and observed the officers at mealtime. Upon seeing them, Mrs. Dunlop asked Britannia, "What would your mother say to this!" "Why Cousin Barbara," Britannia replied, "She would have given me great credit for doing what necessity required. I tell you, you can always maintain your position if you will!"[98]

Like many families of Washington, the Peter-Kennon family was divided by the Civil War. Britannia's stepsons were both Southern sympathizing and fought with the Confederacy. Stepson Bev Kennon resigned his commission in the US Navy the day after Fort Sumter was shelled in April of 1861

age from eighteen to six years old. So, much like her great-grandmother Martha Washington had done a century before and her mother Martha Custis Peter had done fifty years earlier, Britannia stepped in and raised her grandchildren almost as if they were her own children, the youngest three even returning to live with her at Tudor Place.

In the flurry of patriotism surrounding the celebration of the nation's centennial in 1876 and the formation of lineage organizations, including the Daughters of the American Revolution and the Colonial Dames of America, Britannia was highly sought after for membership in these organizations as the only living great-grandchild of Martha Washington. Earlier in her life she had met Lafayette as well as presidents Andrew Jackson, Martin Van Buren, William Henry Harrison, and a number of other prominent figures of American history. Her lineage as a descendant of both the Custis and Calvert families and these interactions with historical and patriotic figures of American history made Britannia Kennon a direct link to the colonial past for these membership organizations. Britannia also lent objects from her personal collection to several exhibitions and, in one instance when she felt that her Washington objects were too valuable to lend, contributed photographs for an exhibition that took place at New York's Metropolitan Opera House in 1889 commemorating the centennial of President Washington's inauguration.[105] Britannia was also visited by reporters to whom she recounted details of Lafayette's visit to Tudor Place and other historical events that she had witnessed in her lifetime in Georgetown. In 1890 the *Century Illustrated Monthly Magazine* published a lengthy article on Britannia and her collection of Washington objects at Tudor Place, titled "Some New Washington Relics in the Collection of Mrs. B. W. Kennon." The author noted, among other things, that that the writing table used by Britannia for her daily correspondence was one that formerly belonged to Martha Washington. Additional Tudor Place objects, including a portrait miniature of Martha Washington and a porcelain plaque of George Washington that Britannia inherited from her parents, were included in another article by art historian Charles Henry Hart titled "Original Portraits of Washington," which appeared in the *Century Magazine* in February 1892.

That same year Britannia received a "perpetual pass" allowing her free entry to Mount Vernon.[106] In the summer of 1893, Britannia was invited to attend Virginia Day, the August 9 celebration held at the World's Columbian Exposition in Chicago. She made the trip accompanied by her grandchildren Freeland and Agnes, spending a week at the fair and enjoying the celebration that took place at the Virginia building, an exact replica of Mount Vernon constructed specifically for the exposition. The day after the Virginia Day celebration, the *Chicago Tribune* noted that among those attending the festivities was "Mrs. Britannia Kennon, the oldest and nearest surviving relative to George Washington."[107] Following the visit to Chicago, Britannia traveled east to Buffalo, New York, where she was finally able to visit the grave of her sister America, who had died there fifty years earlier.

The next year, in the spring of 1894, Britannia traveled to New York City to witness the marriage of her grandson Armistead Peter Jr. to Anna Wright Williams, his

This photograph of Britannia and her grandsons was taken in 1890 to accompany an article about her collection of Washington objects for the *Century Illustrated Monthly Magazine*. Tudor Place Archives.

Britannia Kennon was photographed at Mount Vernon during a visit on July 4, 1892.
Collection of the Mount Vernon Ladies' Association.

Britannia's mother, Martha Parke Custis Peter, received this portrait miniature of her step-grandfather, George Washington, as a wedding present in 1795. It was later inherited by Britannia and is now part of the Tudor Place Collection. Photograph by Bruce White.

distant cousin and her great-niece. Britannia was not one to be slowed down by advancing age—even as she entered her eightieth year in 1895. Her account books listing her expenditures on streetcar tickets that year suggest she was not one to sit idly at home but rather was frequently out and about in the city. She was in the habit of walking to Christ Church, two blocks from Tudor Place, for weekly services and was also involved in many charitable organizations in Georgetown, including the Louise Home and the Sewing Society of Christ Church.[108]

It was around this time that Britannia's now adult grandchildren began to conduct interviews with her, carefully writing down her responses to questions that they posed about family history or important historical events. During these conversations, she recounted stories of meeting Lafayette and of operating Tudor Place as a boarding house during the Civil War as well as memories of Mount Vernon and her Washington great-grandparents that her own mother had told to her seventy years earlier. Her grandchildren wrote down these reminiscences—the narrative that is transcribed and annotated in this volume.

George Alfred Townsend, a *Washington Post* reporter who visited Tudor Place in 1894, described the seventy-nine-year-old Britannia as "tall and slender and silver-crowned," going on to note that she moved "with the delicate poise of a colonial belle dancing the minuet."[109] That same year, a distant cousin remarked in a letter to Britannia that her "fine erect figure, quick easy step, and mental brightness are most uncommon and admirable."[110] In the summer of 1896, Britannia welcomed her first great-grandchild, Armistead Peter 3rd. Britannia

Armistead Peter Jr. took this photograph of his four siblings:
Clockwise from top left: G. Freeland Peter, B. Kennon Peter, Walter G. Peter,
and Agnes Peter at Tudor Place in 1899. Tudor Place Archives.

Britannia Kennon with her great-grandson Armistead Peter 3rd in the Tudor Place Garden, 1910. Tudor Place Archives.

remained in relatively good health for the first decade of the twentieth century. Although she suffered several illnesses serious enough to cause grandson Armistead Peter Jr. to quickly come from New York to be at her bedside, she survived them all. As mobility became a greater issue, she began using an invalid's chair, and photographs taken about six months before her death show her seated in the chair in the Tudor Place garden, surrounded by her grandchildren and her great-grandson.

Britannia Wellington Peter Kennon died in her bedroom at Tudor Place, seated in her favorite chair, on January 27, 1911, one day short of her ninety-sixth birthday. Born at Tudor Place during the administration of the nation's fourth president, James Madison, she took her last breath in the same house more than a decade into the twentieth century during the administration of the twenty-seventh president, William Howard Taft. Over the course of her lifetime, she outlived her parents, her husband, her daughter and son-in-law, both of her stepsons, all of her siblings, and all of the Williams nieces and nephews who had also lived with her at Tudor Place. Britannia's longevity is remarkable, even now in the twenty-first century, but it was especially significant in a century in which medical problems that can today be prevented by a vaccine or remedied with an antibiotic often proved fatal.

Britannia's funeral was held several days after her death, in the Tudor Place drawing room, the same room in which she was married nearly seventy years prior. Following the funeral her remains were taken to Georgetown's Oak Hill Cemetery and placed in the family's plot adjacent to the grave of her husband, whose body had been moved from Congressional Cemetery in

The last formal portrait taken of Britannia Wellington Peter Kennon, ca. 1910. The chair in which she is seated and the cap she is wearing are extant in the Tudor Place collection. Tudor Place Archives.

1874, as well as the graves of her daughter and son-in-law. In a letter written to the Daughters of the American Revolution thanking them for sending an arrangement of flowers to Britannia's funeral, her granddaughter Agnes Peter remarked that she was "always so thoughtful of others; one never heard her complain, her own weariness always being put aside to share our joy."[111]

Britannia Kennon's lasting legacy is the active role she played in the preservation of Tudor Place and the significant collection of objects still found in the house today. In addition to the heirloom objects formerly owned by George and Martha Washington, the Tudor Place collection now includes objects and manuscripts associated with Britannia's nearly sixty years of ownership as well as items related to subsequent generations of the Peter family who also owned the property. Her other legacy is the information that she imparted to her grandchildren—the memories and stories she recounted, which they dutifully recorded and preserved so later generations of the family could know the family's history and the stories behind specific objects in the collection. Britannia instilled her love of history and appreciation for Tudor Place and its collection in both her grandchildren and great-grandchildren. It was Britannia's great-grandson, Armistead Peter 3rd, who created the nonprofit foundation that operates Tudor Place today, allowing the house, gardens, and the significant family collection to be shared with the public. In speaking of his great-grandmother many years later, Armistead 3rd recalled that her "tenacity and perseverance probably did as much as anything in the world to preserve this house to the present day."[112] He also remembered helping her walk from her bedroom to a window in the upper hall where she could look out over the garden. "I have never forgotten the expression of love with which she looked down on that garden," he wrote, "and I am sure it is one of the motivating influences that made me feel that I wanted to do everything I could to put this house and garden back into the condition that they deserved."[113] This proves the lasting impact of Britannia Kennon's legacy even more than sixty years after her death.

1. "Family Record," found written in Martha Custis Peter's Bible, L1984.4632, TPA.

2. Anna Maria Thornton, diary entry, January 29, 1815, Anna Maria Brodeau Thornton Diary, Papers of Anna Maria Thornton, Manuscript Division, Library of Congress.

3. Eliza Quincy to Miss Storer, February 23, 1810, in Quincy, *Memoir of the Life of Eliza S. M. Quincy*, 131.

4. Quincy, *Figures of the Past*, 275–76.

5. Ticknor, *Life, Letters, and Journals of George Ticknor*, 38.

6. Thornton, diary entry, August 24, 1814.

7. Martha Custis Peter to Timothy Pickering, August 28, 1814, Timothy Pickering Papers, Massachusetts Historical Society.

8. Unless otherwise noted, all birth and death dates for the children of Thomas and Martha Peter are taken from the family record found in Martha Peter's Bible in the Tudor Place Archives.

9. Noted in letter by Rosalie Stier Calvert; see Calcott, *Mistress of Riversdale*, 204–5: "Our poor niece, Mrs. Peter is most unlucky with her children. She had a son the age of my Eugene who she lost last year."

10. Noted in the same letter by Rosalie Stier Calvert; see Calcott, *Mistress of Riversdale*, 204–5: "[Mrs. Peter] came to dinner here just day before yesterday and when she returned home, she found her little daughter of seven months somewhat ill. She sent for the doctor and three hours later, the child was no more."

11. Anna Maria Thornton notes in her diary entry of September 23, 1810, that she received a note from "Mrs. Law inclosing [*sic*] one to her f[ro]m Mrs. Peter at Oakland—mentioning the birth & death of an infant."

12. As recounted by Britannia to her grandchildren, see page 118.

13. Robert Peter's letter book is found in the Peter Family Papers, Accession #7605-a, Special Collections, Albert and Shirley Small Special Collections Library, University of Virginia. At the 1911 division of Britannia Kennon's estate, the letter book went to her grandson G. Freeland Peter, whose descendants donated it and other family papers to the University of Virginia in the mid-twentieth century.

14. As Britannia recounted to her grandchildren in February 1896.

15. See Kail, "Oakland."

16. As recounted by Britannia to her grandchildren on February 27, 1905.

17. James Carnahan (1775–1859) operated a classical seminary in Georgetown from 1814 to 1823, leaving Georgetown to assume the presidency of Princeton University, his alma mater.

18. As recounted by Britannia to her grandchildren on June 3, 1896. Bilious colic is a general term for gastric distress that can include attack of gallstones or a rupture of the gallbladder.

19. Eleanor Nelly Custis Lewis to E. B. Gibson, December 4, 1820, quoted in Brady, *George Washington's Beautiful Nelly*, 94–95.

20. As recounted by Britannia to her grandchildren, June 3, 1896.

21. M. C. Peter to E. B. Gibson, December 14, 1820, Papers of Thomas and Martha Peter, MS 2, Box 1, Folder 6, TPA.

22. "A Page from the Life of Lafayette: His Visit to Tudor Place in 1824 Related by the Great Granddaughter of Mrs. Washington," *Washington Times*, July 4, 1895. The text of the article was recopied by Armistead Peter Jr. into one of his compilations of his grandmother's reminiscences.

23. A levee is a gathering or reception.

24. Eleanor "Nelly" Custis Lewis to Georges W. Lafayette, March 5, 1826, Arthur H. and Mary Marden Dean Lafayette Collection, Cornell University Library.

25. See Kail, "George Washington's Great-Granddaughter."

26. Quoted in Kail.

27. Mannard, "'To Raise the Academy to a Standard of Excellence Equal to Any'."

28. As recounted to her grandchildren on February 27, 1905. See page 170.

29. Sullivan, *Georgetown Visitation since 1799*, 192.

30. Mannard, "'To Raise the Academy'."

31. Mannard. As Mannard discusses, Wightt believed that the Ursuline Order was better adapted to American conditions and more supportive of female education. The fourth vow taken by Ursuline sisters was a vow dedicating themselves to female education.

32. Helen Marie Simpson Lueber (1807–1890) of Georgetown. Britannia recounted this information to her grandchildren on March 6, 1905.

33. As recounted by Britannia to her grandchildren on February 13, 1897.

34. Thornton, diary, February 5, 1830.

35. Sarah Elizabeth Peter was born at Tudor Place on February 11, 1831.

36. Thornton, diary, April 30, 1831.

37. Britannia recalled this to her grandchildren on January 28, 1901.

38. She recalled this to her grandson Walter G. Peter. See Peter, "A Collection of Facts Pertaining to the Peter Family in America, the Indians Who Inhabited This Country, and Georgetown on the Potomac," p. 132, photocopy of unpublished and undated typescript, TPA, Archivist's Research Files.

39. Reminiscences of Armistead Peter Jr., undated, Papers of Armistead Peter Jr., MS 14, Box 69, TPA.

40. Mary Lee Fitzhugh Custis to Mary Anna Randolph Custis Lee, January 29 [1839?], Arlington House Manuscripts, #12644. I am grateful to Cassandra Good for bringing this letter to my attention. O'Sullivan was editor of the failed *Metropolitan* newspaper in Georgetown, which was criticized for being the voice of President Andrew Jackson's administration and policies. In 1837 he was founding editor of the *United States Magazine and Democratic Review* in which he later coined the term "Manifest Destiny" as part of an 1845 essay. For more information, see Sampson, *John L. O'Sullivan and His Times*, 8-15.

41. As Britannia recounted to her grandchildren on April 6, 1895.

42. Kennon served as commandant of the Washington Navy Yard from April 27, 1841, to March 7, 1843, after which he was appointed chief of the Navy's Bureau of Construction, Equipment, and Repair. Hibben, *Navy-Yard, Washington*, 19.

43. Kail, "Residence on H Street."

44. Thornton, diary, April 30, 1842.

45. Thornton, diary, April 30, 1842, in Kuniholm, "Transcription of the Diaries of Mrs. William Thornton, 1793–1863," typescript found in the Research Files, Tudor Place Research Library.

46. Thornton, diary, April 30, 1842, in Kuniholm typescript.

47. As recounted to her grandchildren on January 16, 1897.

48. Beverley Kennon to Rev. Mr. Hoff, December 6, 1842, Papers of Britannia W. Kennon, Peter Family Papers, Mount Vernon Library.

49. Thornton, diary, December 9, 1842.

50. Marolda, *Washington Navy Yard*, 6.

51. Sharp, *History of the Washington Navy Yard Civilian Workforce*, 5.

52. Sharp, 5.

53. Hibben, *Navy-Yard, Washington*, 74–77.

54. Short, *Development of National Administrative Organization in the United States*, 167.

55. Kail, "Residence on H Street."

56. As indicated by a November 21, 1843, letter addressed to Britannia at Tudor Place from her husband in which he provides details of events that occurred on his side of Rock Creek.

57. Thornton, diary, October 18, 1843.

58. Martha Williams Carter, Britannia's niece, included a full account of the day in her diary and in letters to several family members. See Scott and Webb, *Who Is Markie*, 23.

59. As cited in Scott and Webb, 23.

60. Scott and Webb.

61. Blackman, "Fatal Cruise of the Princeton," 39.

62. Pearson, "The 'Princeton' and the 'Peacemaker,'" 179–80.

63. Martha Custis Williams letter, as cited in Scott and Webb, *Who Is Markie*, 23–24.

64. President John Tyler to Britannia W. Kennon, March 4, 1844, Peter Family Papers, Papers of Britannia W. Kennon, Mount Vernon Library.

65. "The Late Calamitous Accident," *National Intelligencer*, March 1, 1844, p. 1, TPA.

66. Francis Blair to Andrew Jackson, March 2, 1844, Andrew Jackson Papers: Series 1, General Correspondence and Related Items, Manuscript Division, LOC.

67. In 1874 the bodies of Commodore Beverley Kennon and Secretary of the Navy Abel P. Upshur were moved from the Congressional Cemetery to Georgetown's Oak Hill Cemetery.

68. Clarke, *Life and Letters of Dolly* [sic] *Madison*, 334.

69. Last Will and Testament of Beverley Kennon, January 1, 1844, Papers of Beverley Kennon, MS 8, Box 1, TPA.

70. Copy of this advertisement found in the Papers of Britannia W. Kennon, MS 7, Box 2, TPA.

71. "Negroes sold for" document found in the Papers of Britannia W. Kennon, MS 7, Box 2, TPA.

72. As cited in Scott and Webb, *Who Is Markie*, 24.

73. Diary of Martha Custis Williams Carter, 1844, Arlington House, Transcription in the Research Files, Curator's Office, Tudor Place Historic House & Garden. Reverend Butler served as rector of St. John's Episcopal Church from September 16, 1841, to April 7, 1844. Martha Custis Kennon appears in the 1844 record of baptisms in St. John's Parish, Georgetown, DC.

74. Brady, *George Washington's Beautiful Nelly*, 241.

75. Britannia Kennon Account Book, March 1844 to March 1845, Papers of Britannia W. Kennon, MS 7, Box 3, TPA.

76. As recounted by Britannia to her grandchildren on April 4, 1895.

77. "Death of a Distinguished Lady," *Evening Star* [Washington, DC], November 10, 1854, p. 3.

78. Thornton, diary, July 13, 1854: "My old friend Mrs. Peter departed at one o'clock this morning."

79. Debutts, *Growing Up in the 1850s*, 40–41.

80. Thornton, diary, November 25, 1853.

81. A bill from 1857 for payment of a gas tax survives in Britannia's papers, TPA.

82. As recounted to her grandchildren on May 11, 1900.

83. Martha Custis Kennon to Britannia W. Kennon, December 18, 1858, Papers of Britannia W. Kennon, MS 7, Box 1, TPA.

84. Thornton, diary, November 10, 1854.

85. An annotated version of this letter appears in Torrance, "Arlington and Mount Vernon 1856," 153.

86. "Family List" Christ Church Registers, Vol. 2, 1866–1875, Transcription found in research files, Curator's Office, Tudor Place.

87. In Torrance, "Arlington and Mount Vernon 1856," 156.

88. Biographical Statement of Beverley Kennon Jr., Papers of Armistead Peter Jr., MS 14, Box 57, TPA.

89. Lomax, *Leaves from an Old Washington Diary*, 71.

90. A notice in the May 10, 1856, issue of the *Washington Union* newspaper notes, "Tudor Place For Rent. This well-known, beautiful residence is offered for rent for a term of years."

91. As Britannia recounted to her grandchildren in an undated passage found on page 176.

92. The pressed flowers are found in an envelope on which Markie noted the day she received them. They are found in her papers, MS 10, Box 1, TPA.

93. As recounted to her grandchildren on February 26, 1897.

94. Kail, "Tudor Place and the Civil War Home Front."

95. Records of the Provost Marshall for Fort Monroe indicate that "Mrs. Beverly Kennon" and "Miss Kennon" were aboard a "flag of truce" boat that arrived at the fort on December 5, 1861. "Office of the Provost Marshall, Fort Monroe [Virginia], December 6, 1861," Union Citizens File, NARA, RG 109, Roll 153, accessed via Fold3.com.

96. As recounted to her grandchildren on February 26, 1897.

97. As recounted to her grandchildren on February 26, 1897.

98. As recounted to her grandchildren on December 16, 1904.

99. "Biographical Statement of Beverley Kennon, Jr."

100. Undated recollection from Armistead Peter Jr. about his father's Civil War service. Papers of Armistead Peter Jr., TPA.

101. As cited in Scott and Webb, *Who Is Markie*, 121.

102. Burial Records for Lot 544, Oak Hill Cemetery, Copy in the Research Files, Curator's Office, Tudor Place.

103. Peter, *Tudor Place*, 29.

104. "In Memoriam: Martha Custis Kennon," Memorial Booklet containing the text of Rev. A. R. Stuart's 1886 funeral homily in which he stated, "Mrs. Peter was found at an early hour, by her little son Freeland, quietly sleeping, with folded hands and head softly pillowed, the sleep which has no waking here." Papers of Dr. Armistead Peter, MS 13, Box 5.

105. A listing of the photographs can be found in the *Catalogue of the Loan Exhibition of Historical Portraits and Relics, Metropolitan Opera House, New York City, April 17th to May 8th, 1889* (New York, 1889). Many of these actual photographs displayed for the exhibit also survive and are now in the Peter Family Papers at the University of Virginia's Albert and Shirley Small Special Collections Library.

106. In the spring of 1892 Justine Townsend sent Britannia a "perpetual pass for Mount Vernon." In the accompanying letter, Townsend wrote, "I hope that you and your family will often visit your old ancestral home. The dear grandchildren ought to go weekly. Mrs. Justine Townsend to Britannia W. Kennon, April 5, 1892, Papers of Britannia W. Kennon, MS 7, Box 1, TPA.

107. "Virginia Day," *Chicago Tribune*, August 10, 1893.

108. She recounted to her grandchildren a complete listing of the charitable organizations in which she held leadership positions on January 11, 1897.

109. George Alfred Townsend, "Linked to Mount Vernon: A Talk with Martha Washington's Great-granddaughter," *Washington Post*, February 26, 1893, copied by Walter G. Peter in his "Collection of Facts Pertaining to the Peter Family in America," 146.

110. Ella Bassett Washington to Britannia W. Kennon, July 16, 1894, Papers of Britannia W. Kennon, MS 7, Box 1, TPA.

111. Agnes Peter to the Daughters of the American Revolution, February 4, 1911, as printed in the "Minutes of the National Board of Management, N.S.D.A.R.," *American Monthly Magazine* 39, no. 1 (July 1911): 31.

112. Peter, *Tudor Place*, 41.

113. Peter, 42.

THE REMINISCENCES OF

Britannia Wellington Peter Kennon

After the Revolutionary War, General Lafayette paid a visit to General Washington at Mount Vernon in 1784 and it was there that my mother, then a child of seven summers, met that great and good man at the house of her grandmother, Mrs. Washington.[16]

The four grandchildren were staying there at the time, and there can be no doubt that he was fond of little ones; for after his return to France he sent a memento to each of them: a quaint little writing desk, complete in all of its appointments was his present to my mother, little Martha Custis—"from her friend General Lafayette."[17]

The child little thought that in later years she would welcome the giver to her own home, and that he should there see the great-grandchild of Mrs. Washington, but such was the case, for in 1824, Lafayette, with his son George Washington Lafayette, and his friend Auguste Levasseur, visited the United States as the Nation's guests.[18]

Such a change as had taken place! That Lafayette did not expect to

16. Marie-Joseph Paul Yves Roch Gilbert du Motier, Marquis de Lafayette (1757–1834) was a French officer who served under Gen. George Washington during the American Revolution. In 1824 President James Monroe invited Lafayette to return to the United States for a goodwill tour. Lafayette visited Mount Vernon in August 1784, staying for ten days. Martha Custis Peter (1777–1854), Britannia's mother, was the second eldest daughter of John Parke Custis and Eleanor Calvert Custis. Martha was born in the blue room at Mount Vernon on December 31, 1777.

17. The grandchildren were Martha Custis Peter and her three siblings: Elizabeth "Eliza" Parke Custis Law (1776–1831), George Washington Parke Custis (1781–1857), and Eleanor "Nelly" Custis Lewis (1779–1852). This small writing desk is extant and in the private collection of one of Britannia Kennon's descendants.

18. Lafayette's son, Georges Washington Motier de Lafayette (1779–1849), accompanied him on the 1824–25 tour of the United States. André-Nicolas Levasseur, also known as Auguste Levasseur (1795–1878), served as Lafayette's personal secretary during the 1824–25 tour. In 1829 Levasseur published his travel notes and memoirs from the trip as *Lafayette en Amérique, en 1824 et 1825 ou Journal d'un voyage aux États-Unis*. He later served the French government in diplomatic posts in Haiti and Mexico.

see the march of improvement was evident, from a remark he made on board ship as to the probability of his being able to hire a carriage to take him to the hotel. On arriving in New York City, he found a coach and four waiting to convey them to the house of George Clinton, then Vice President of the United States.[19]

After leaving New York he visited Boston, Philadelphia, and Baltimore before coming to Washington.[20] On arriving at the District line, he was met by military companies from Washington, Alexandria, and Georgetown who escorted him to the gate to the Capitol.[21] He was there met by twenty-five young girls, clad in white, representing the twenty-four states and the District of Columbia. The one representing the later place stepped forward and delivered a speech of welcome.[22] Passing into the rotunda of the Capitol, the General held a reception at which I was present with my parents.[23]

After the reception the Mayor of Washington gave an address, and then presented him to the Mayor of Georgetown, Colonel John Cox, who extended an invitation from the

19. Lafayette and his entourage arrived in New York City on August 14, 1824. His arrival in New York was announced in the August 18, 1824, issue of Washington's *National Intelligencer* newspaper. Here Britannia incorrectly identifies George Clinton (1739–1812) as vice president at the time of Lafayette's 1824 visit, but Clinton had died in office in 1812 while serving as President Madison's vice president. At the time of Lafayette's 1824 visit, Daniel Tompkins (1774–1825), also of New York, was vice president.

20. Lafayette was in Boston, Massachusetts, from August 25 to August 31, 1824. Lafayette arrived in Philadelphia on September 28, 1824. During this visit a parade was held and speeches given in his honor at the Pennsylvania State House. Lafayette was in Baltimore, Maryland, from October 8 to 11, 1824. While in the city he met with surviving veterans of the American Revolution. Lafayette arrived in Washington on October 12, 1824.

21. After being escorted from Baltimore by Samuel Sprigg, former governor of Maryland, and by a volunteer cavalry, Lafayette crossed from Maryland into the District of Columbia.

22. According to the October 15, 1824, issue of the *National Intelligencer* newspaper, Miss Sarah M. Watterston represented the District of Columbia and delivered the welcome speech. Dixon, *National Intelligencer Abstracts, 1824–26,* 128.

23. Britannia notes that she accompanied her parents to the October 14, 1824, reception at the Capitol Building.

citizens to visit the latter place, which he accepted, saying, "Georgetown is an old friend of mine, and I shall visit it with pleasure."[24]

That same evening, after a dinner given by President James Monroe he begged that he might be permitted to retire in order that he might pay a visit in Georgetown to some intimate friends and connections to the family of General Washington.[25]

He drove to Tudor Place in a private carriage. I can see the grand man now as he entered the door of the Parlor; his genial manner and dignified appearance making an impression

24. Roger Chew Weightman (1787–1876) was mayor of Washington, DC, during the time of Lafayette's visit. John Cox (1775–1849), a merchant and militia colonel, was mayor of Georgetown in 1824. He held the office from 1823 until 1845.

25. James Monroe (1758–1836) served as president of the United States from 1817 to 1825. Monroe hosted a dinner for Lafayette at the President's House on the evening of October 13, 1824.

When Lafayette visited Tudor Place in October 1824, he presented this engraving to Thomas and Martha Peter. Collection of Tudor Place Historic House & Garden, photograph by Bruce White.

on my mind which time cannot efface.[26] Advancing to my mother, he tenderly embraced her, the meeting no doubt bringing to his mind recollections of former days when he had known her as a child, romping over the lawns of Mt. Vernon, the guest of his everlasting friend, George Washington. After leaving my mother, he paid a visit to her sister, Mrs. E. P. Custis, who was then living at Peter Grove.[27]

A few evenings later, he with his son, and friend Auguste Levasseur, dined with my parents, Mr. and Mrs. Thomas Peter at Tudor Place where other guests had been invited to meet him.[28] While in Washington, at the invitation of the Mayor of Georgetown, General Lafayette and his party visited Georgetown College and afterwards attended a reception given at Col. Cox's house, where the following incident occurred:[29] Among the guests was Anna Key, daughter of Francis Scott Key, author of "The Star Spangled Banner."[30] She was a great admirer of General Lafayette and as she came quickly into the room where he was, she dropped on her knee, and kissing his hand, was gone, as she had

26. Britannia was nine years old when Lafayette visited Tudor Place in October 1824.

27. "Mrs. E. P. Custis" is Elizabeth "Eliza" Parke Custis Law (1776–1831), Britannia's aunt. At the time of Lafayette's visit, she was renting "Peter Grove," a house on R Street in Georgetown. "Peter Grove" was the estate of David Peter (1778–1812), Britannia's uncle. Located on Road [now R] Street, about three blocks from Tudor Place, the property was leased to several tenants after the deaths of David Peter and his wife.

28. Georges Washington Motier de Lafayette (1779–1849), and Levasseur, Lafayette's personal secretary. See note 18.

29. The mayor of Georgetown was John Cox. See note 24. Founded in 1789 as Georgetown College, Georgetown University has been located in western Georgetown since the late eighteenth century. Lafayette's October 14 visit to the campus was reported in the October 19, 1824, issue of the *National Intelligencer*. Dixon, *National Intelligencer Abstracts, 1824–1826*, 130–32. Col. John Cox and his wife, Elizabeth, resided at The Cedars, an estate in upper Georgetown. However, the October 14, 1824, dinner that Cox hosted for Lafayette was held in one of the empty dwellings on Cox's Row, a group of townhouses owned by Colonel Cox located on the corner of 34th Street and N Street NW. The change in location was because Mrs. Cox was at home and overdue to deliver a child. See Ecker, *Portrait of Old Georgetown*, 127.

30. Ann Arnold Key Turner (1811–1884), daughter of Francis Scott Key, married Rep. Daniel Turner of North Carolina in 1829. Francis Scott Key (1779–1843), a Georgetown lawyer and poet, is best known as the author of a poem, "Defence of Fort M'Henry," that was later set to music and adopted as the National Anthem of the United States.

West Point and then to the White Mountains for the Summer. We were boarding at Mrs. Abbot's on West St., the place ("Tudor") being rented at the time to the Pendletons.[57] The war broke out just then and instead of going North, as we had thought of doing, we packed our trunks and went to Staunton, Virginia.

The Pendletons rented "Tudor" in the Summer of 1858 and I came back in 1862 on January 1st.[58] She was very wealthy, having first married a Mr. Cox, an old man, by whom she got her fortune.[59] Mr. Pendleton, her second husband, was a Virginian and was poor when he married her.[60]

I had stored my furniture in rooms at the Seminary Building.[61] In 1861 (while I was in Virginia) the Government took, among other places, that building for a hospital and ordered everything moved out at once.[62] Cousin Robert Dick and Doctor Riley remembered that I had things stored there and kindly got wagons and had everything hauled pell-mell to Bridge St. and stored in one of Mrs. Abbot's houses.[63] From Georgetown we went to Staunton

57. P Street NW was known as West Street prior to 1895; see appendix 1. In 1858 Britannia leased Tudor Place to William Armistead Pendleton, and she rented rooms for herself in a house owned by Mrs. Abbot, a Georgetown widow who lived at 3014 West Street (now P Street), at the southeast corner of West and Washington [30th] Streets.

58. During the time that William Armistead Pendleton (1825–70) rented Tudor Place, several members of his immediate and extended family resided on the property. According to the 1860 US Census, Pendleton; his wife, Mary Ann Pendleton (1827–90); their three children, William Jr. (1860–1916), Ida (1860–1937), and Mary (1857–92); and William's widower father, John Lewis Pendleton (1790/92–1869), along with four white servants and four enslaved individuals, were living at Tudor Place.

59. Mrs. Pendleton was the daughter of Maj. Taylor Berry of St. Louis, Missouri. In 1837 she married Henry Sidney Coxe in St. Louis. He died in 1850, and three years later she married William Armistead Pendleton in St. Louis on February 7, 1853. Henry Sidney Coxe (1798–1850) was cashier at the Bank of the United States in St. Louis, Missouri.

60. William Armistead Pendleton (1825–70) was the son of John L. Pendleton and Eliza Bankhead Magruder Pendleton. A native of Caroline County, Virginia, he practiced law in Washington, DC, during the time he leased Tudor Place from Britannia Kennon.

61. The Seminary Building was located at the corner of Washington and Gay Streets (30th and N Streets) in Georgetown. It was previously the home of Miss English's Seminary and later the Georgetown Female Seminary.

62. The Union Army confiscated the Seminary Building in July 1861 for use as an officer's hospital.

63. Robert Dick (1800–1870), Britannia's first cousin, was the son of Margaret Peter Dick and Thomas Dick. Dr. Joshua Riley (1800–1875) was a Georgetown physician. Dr. Armistead Peter, Britannia's son-in-law, was a pupil of Dr. Riley's when he studied medicine. Bridge Street is the Georgetown street now known as M Street NW. It was so named because it was the location of a bridge that crossed Rock Creek, the body of water separating Georgetown from the rest of Washington, DC. See appendix 1 for a list of Georgetown street names prior to the 1895 renaming.

After the outbreak of the Civil War, Britannia and her daughter traveled through Virginia, living in Staunton, Richmond, Petersburg, and Norfolk. Britannia returned to Georgetown and Tudor Place on January 1, 1862. Tudor Place Archives.

where we stayed from April to the middle of July, boarding at Mrs. [Lomax's] Private house.[64] After General Garret's defeat, we thought that the "Yankees" would come to Staunton so we went down to Richmond.[65] One of the first persons I met on Main St. was Cousin Robert Lee.[66] "Well, Cousin Brit, what brought you down here!" said Cousin Robert, "To put myself under your protection!" We stayed at Mrs. Dabney's boarding house until the middle of November.[67] Money got short and we went to Petersburg, where we remained one month; boarding with Mrs. Page, who kept a private boarding house.[68] We were "Refugees"—and very poor. Winter came on and we had no flannels. Cousin [left blank] gave me one flannel skirt.

At the end of the month, fearing that the Government might take "Tudor" for a hospital, we decided to return home. We went to Norfolk.[69] Terry Sinclair met us there and we stayed at his house for two days.[70] He saw General Huger for me and asked whether we could not come up in the first "flag of truce."[71] The General and

64. Staunton, now an independent city in Augusta County, Virginia, is located in the Shenandoah Valley. The name of the owner of the boarding house is left blank in all versions of Britannia Kennon's Reminiscences found in the Tudor Place Archives. However, she is later identified by Armistead Peter Jr. in another document as the home of Britannia's friend, Elizabeth Virginia Lindsay Lomax (1796–1867). See Kail, "Tudor Place and the Civil War Home Front."

65. Confederate general Robert S. Garrett was defeated at the Battle of Cheat Mountain in Pocahontas and Randolph Counties, Virginia (now West Virginia), in September 1861. This battle occurred less than seventy-five miles from Staunton, and residents feared that the Union Army would push east into the Shenandoah Valley following this victory. Britannia's appearance in Richmond is mentioned in a letter that Agnes Lee wrote to her sister Mildred on August 20, 1861: "Cousin Brit & Markie are boarding in Richmond both looking very well." See Lee Family Papers, Mss1 L51 c 380, Section 19, Virginia Historical Society, Richmond. Transcribed and accessed on the Lee Family Digital Archive, https://leefamilyarchive.org.

66. Britannia Kennon always referred to Robert E. Lee as "Cousin Robert" because he was married to her first cousin Mary Custis Lee.

67. Advertisements in the *Richmond Dispatch* from this time period indicate that a Mrs. Dabney was letting rooms in her home located on the corner of Franklin and 3rd Streets in Richmond.

68. This was probably Caroline Matilda Page (1818–97), a widow who resided in Petersburg at 62 High Street. Page's husband, William Armistead Page, died in 1855.

69. Norfolk, Virginia, is located adjacent to Hampton Roads, a large natural harbor at the mouth of the Chesapeake Bay.

70. Terry Sinclair (1816–85) was the nephew of Britannia Kennon's late husband, Cdre. Beverley Kennon. Sinclair was a Norfolk native and officer in the US Navy who resigned his commission in April 1861 to join the Confederate Navy. He was a member of the wedding party when Britannia married Beverley in 1842 and also had a son who was Markie's age. The Sinclair house was located at 6 Washington Street in Norfolk, according to *Vickery's Directory of the City of Norfolk.* Ferslew, *Vicker's Directory*, 115.

71. Gen. Benjamin Huger (1805–77), the Confederate commander of the Department of Norfolk, was responsible for the defense of coastal North Carolina and southern Virginia. "Flag of Truce" boats transported passengers from the Confederate-held portions of Norfolk across Hampton Roads to Union-controlled Fort Monroe.

Mrs. Huger called on us that evening and in two days we took the boat, being the only passengers on board, save a culprit.[72] We took the Confederate boat at Norfolk and were met in mid-water by the Federal "flag of truce" boat where we were transferred. When we arrived at Fortress Monroe nearly everyone went ashore but your Mother and I, being "Confederates," were kept on board.[73] Reporters came on board and tried to get news from us but failed. That night at Fortress Monroe an officer came to me and said he was obliged to search our baggage, saying, that it was not an agreeable duty but necessity required it. I told he was welcome to search our trunks and handed him the keys. He opened my trunk, looked at one tray and shut the lid. I told there were other trays but he was satisfied to take my word and went no further. We arrived at Baltimore the next morning and went immediately to Brother's where we stayed one week. I left your dear Mother there and came to "Tudor," arriving at home on January 1st 1862.[74]

72. The general's wife was Elizabeth Celestine Pinckney Huger (1805–82).

73. Located on Old Point Comfort, Fort Monroe was used by the Union Army to guard the navigation channel between Hampton Roads and the Chesapeake Bay as well as the mouth of the Chesapeake Bay, which empties into the Atlantic Ocean. "Your Mother" refers to Martha "Markie" Kennon. Records of the Provost Marshall for Fort Monroe indicate that "Mrs. Beverly Kennon" and "Miss Kennon" were on board a "flag of truce" boat that arrived at the fort on December 5, 1861. Union Citizens File, NARA, RG 109, accessed via Fold3.com.

74. Britannia Kennon returned to Tudor Place on January 1, 1862, after leaving Markie at Lynwood, her brother George Washington Peter's Howard County, Maryland, estate.

The Last time General Lee visited the District he stayed here at "Tudor Place," and if I recollect alright, he occupied this very room (now Grandmother's bedroom).[96] When Cousin Robert came to "Tudor" I told him how glad I was to see him and he said: "Well, Cousin Brit, I have come to spend one more night at "Tudor Place" before I die!"—He stayed two days, if not three, spending Sunday with us. It was a rainy, disagreeable day and I suggested, as the weather was so bad, we would not go to church in the morning but, if the weather cleared, we would go at night, which we did, Cousin Robert accompanying me. The Rev. Mr. Williams (the Rector of Christ Church) was very much disappointed that we did

96. Lee visited Washington, DC, in May of 1869.

Britannia called Robert E. Lee "Cousin Robert" after his 1831 marriage to her cousin Mary Anna Custis. Britannia owned this signed *carte de visite* of Lee taken by Washington photographer Alexander Gardner in 1866. Tudor Place Archives.

not come to the morning service, it being Communion Sunday—he had hoped to administer the Sacraments to General Lee.[97] The congregation was disappointed also for they had hoped to see him in the morning.[98]

During his stay at "Tudor" Cousin Robert called at the White House and paid his respects to President Grant, saying, he felt it was his duty to do so.[99]

February 13, 1897

I was at several entertainments at Daniel Webster's (now the Corcoran House, it was a single house then).[100] Mrs. Webster was a splendid looking woman, not beautiful but tall and commanding.[101] I was at one of their entertainments when Lord Morpeth was entertained there.[102]

97. Rev. Walter Wheeler Williams (1834–92) was rector of Christ Episcopal Church from 1866 to 1876. Christ Episcopal Church is located two blocks south of the Tudor Place property at the corner of 31st and O Streets in Georgetown.

98. This line is included in the original handwritten notes taken by Armistead Peter Jr. of his conversation with his grandmother but omitted from later typescripts that he prepared.

99. During the visit to Washington, Lee called at the White House and met with President Ulysses S. Grant on May 1, 1869. This was their first meeting since the April 9, 1865, meeting at Appomattox Court House to discuss terms of surrender. At the time of the 1869 visit, Lee was serving as president of Washington College (now Washington & Lee University) in Lexington, Virginia.

100. Daniel Webster (1782–1852) served as representative, senator, and later secretary of state. He rented and eventually purchased a three-story house adjacent to Lafayette Square at the corner of H Street and Connecticut Avenue NW. Originally constructed in 1828 by Thomas Swann, Webster owned the property from 1840 to 1848. Financier W. W. Corcoran purchased the federal townhouse from Webster in 1848 and hired architect James Renwick Jr. to transform it into a grand Italianate palazzo. In 1922 the house was demolished for the construction of the U.S. Chamber of Commerce Building that now stands on this block. See Goode, *Capital Losses*, 54; and MacKay, "Corcoran Mansion."

101. Daniel Webster's second wife was Caroline LeRoy Webster (1797–1882), whom he married on December 18, 1829.

102. George W. F. Howard Carlisle, Lord Morpeth (1802–64), was a member of Parliament and later the 7th Earl of Carlisle, Knight of the Garter and Privy councilor to Queen Victoria. Styled Viscount Morpeth from 1825 to 1848, he visited Washington as part of a tour of the United States in 1842. Webster was previously acquainted with Morpeth from his 1839 tour of England. See Paige, *Daniel Webster in England*, 143. Morpeth was in Washington in late January of 1842. The *National Intelligencer* noted on January 20, 1842, "Among the strangers now visiting Washington City is Lord Morpeth a distinguished British Statesman." Dixon, *National Intelligencer Abstracts, 1842*, 23.

I also knew John C. Calhoun, then Secretary of War, and his family.[103] He lived with his mother at what is now the Linthicum Place.[104] Anna Maria Calhoun took dancing lessons with me in this very room (*Grandmother's*

103. John C. Calhoun (1782–1850) of South Carolina served as secretary of war during President James Monroe's administration from 1817 to 1825. He later served as vice president of the United States from 1825 to 1832, resigning the position to return to the Senate. From 1822 to 1829, Calhoun and his family lived across R Street from the Tudor Place property on the estate now known as Dumbarton Oaks. Edward Linthicum purchased the property in 1846, and that is why Britannia refers to it as the "Linthicum Place" in this paragraph.

104. Actually, he lived with his mother-in-law, Floride Rebecca Bonneau Colhoun (1770–1836), widow of South Carolina senator John Ewing Colhoun (see note 534). John C. Calhoun's mother, Martha Caldwell Calhoun, died in South Carolina in 1802. The property, known after 1922 as Dumbarton Oaks, across R Street, was previously known by other names given to it by prior owners, including Acrolophos, Monterey, The Oaks, and Oakly. In 1940 owners Mr. and Mrs. Robert Woods Bliss gave Dumbarton Oaks to Harvard University.

Secretary of war and later vice president John C. Calhoun and his family owned the property across the street from Tudor Place. Britannia recalled taking dancing lessons with his daughter Anna Maria. *John C. Calhoun* by Charles Bird King, ca. 1823. National Portrait Gallery, Smithsonian Institution; gift of the A. W. Mellon Educational and Charitable Trust.

bed-room by the quarter [105]).[106] There was Mildred Lee, Cousin Robert's youngest sister; Caroline Mackall, Henrietta Dunlop, Anna Maria Calhoun and myself.[107] Mr. DuPort came up here and played his fiddle and taught us steps.[108] Mother found that those girls wanted to join a private class and Mr. DuPort said if she would get up a class he would teach us and that's the way I knew Anna Maria so well.[109]

105. Britannia's grandchildren, including Armistead Peter Jr., who included this parenthetical aside, would have been familiar with the room on the second floor of the West Wing of Tudor Place in which Britannia recalled taking the dancing lessons because, during their childhood in the 1870s, it was the room in which she resided, which is why it is noted here as "grandmother's bedroom by the quarter."

106. Anna Maria Calhoun Clemson (1817–75) was the daughter of John C. and Floride Colhoun Calhoun. In 1838, Anna Maria married Thomas Green Clemson, who later founded South Carolina's Clemson University. For a biography of Anna C. Clemson, see Russell, *Legacy of a Southern Lady*.

107. Catherine Mildred Lee Childe (1811–56) was the youngest daughter of Henry "Light-Horse Harry" Lee and Anne Hill Carter Lee. She married Edward Vernon Childe in 1831. Caroline Mackall Duvall (1820–66) was the daughter of Benjamin Mackall and Christiana Beall Mackall of Georgetown. In 1862 Caroline married Matthew Duvall of Prince George's County, Maryland. Henrietta J. Dunlop (1813–93), Britannia's first cousin, was the daughter of James and Elizabeth Peter Dunlop. When Britannia married Beverley Kennon in 1842, Henrietta was a member of the wedding party.

108. Pierre Landrin Duport (1762–1841) was a dancing instructor in Georgetown. Claiming to have taught the children of Marie Antoinette, he fled France three days after the fall of the Bastille and arrived in Philadelphia in 1790, later producing ballets and teaching dance in Philadelphia, New York, and Baltimore. By 1812 he settled in Georgetown. Receipts from Duport for Britannia's dancing lessons in 1826 and 1828 survive in the Peter Family Papers at the Fred W. Smith National Library for the Study of George Washington at Mount Vernon. For biographical information on Duport, see Keller, "Pierre Landrin DuPort."

109. "Mother" is Martha Custis Peter, Britannia's mother.

"Peter Grove" was built by Uncle David Peter.[110] The house was a good deal the style of "Tudor Place" having three rooms to the south and a hallway along the north. There was only the main building, a corridor, and one wing. It was occupied by them and their two daughters were married from there.[111] After their death it was rented.[112] Aunt Law lived there for some time and it was while she lived there in 1824 that Lafayette dined there.[113]

The place was afterward sold and Mr. Carter (a Representative from South Carolina I think) purchased it.[114] He built another corridor and wing to the main building and improved the place greatly. He had one daughter who married Colonel O'Neal.[115] They had a son, Carter O'Neal to who the place belonged after his mother's death. He was educated in England and later joined the British army.[116] On coming of age he came to this country and sold the place to Henry D. Cooke.[117]

110. David Peter (1778–1812), Britannia's uncle, owned Peter Grove, an estate located on Road Street (present day R Street) about two blocks from the Tudor Place property in Georgetown. He died in 1812 at age thirty-four.

111. David Peter and his wife, Sarah Johns Peter, had seven children, four of whom survived infancy. The two daughters married at Peter Grove were Jane Johns Peter (1800–1863), who married James Bradshaw Beverley, the son of neighbor Robert Beverley, on May 6, 1819, and Elizabeth Margaret Peter (1804–37), who married William Wilson Ramsay on October 15, 1822.

112. Sarah Johns Peter survived her husband David Peter (d. 1812), dying on October 7, 1823.

113. Aunt Law is Elizabeth "Eliza" Parke Custis Law (1776–1831), Britannia's aunt. Eliza married Thomas Law in 1795, but the couple separated in 1804 and divorced in 1811.

114. John Carter (1792–1850) was a former South Carolina representative. Carter purchased the Peter Grove property from John Marbury in 1844. Carter expanded the house and renamed the estate "Carolina Place" in an allusion to his home state. See Gordon, "Old Homes on Georgetown Heights," 83.

115. Ann Eliza Carter O'Neal (1819–46), the daughter of Col. John Carter, married Thomas Whitfoot O'Neal (1812–69) of Barbados in 1842. Ann died in 1846, and their son, John Carter O'Neal, inherited the property when he came of age.

116. Maj. John Carter O'Neal (1845–1909) served in the British army with the Inniskilling Dragoons. He later served as justice of the peace for the English county of Leicester.

117. O'Neal sold the property to Henry David Cooke (1825–81) in 1867. Cooke was a partner in the financial firm Jay Cooke & Co. and manager of their Washington office. He also became president of the Washington and Georgetown Street Railway Company in 1862. President Grant later appointed Cooke to be the first territorial governor of the District of Columbia, an office he held from 1871 to 1873.

About 1862 or '63, while belonging to Carter O'Neal, Sartiges the French minister, was living there, when the house took fire and burned to the ground.[118]

January 16, 1897

The Reverend Mr. Brook (I think) the pastor of Christ Church (St. John's Church, Georgetown, being closed) objected to any one being confirmed in his church who would not give up dancing—so Sister America and I were confirmed in St. John's church, Washington, D.C. (the Reverend Mr. Hawley being the rector) about 1840.[119]

Could Mr. Hawley come back to his old church now I hardly think he would feel at home or know what to do for the changes have been so great.[120] He and old Mr. Laird (Mr. Laird Jr.'s grandfather) were the last two old gentlemen who I remember wearing knee breeches.[121] The Rev. Mr. Hawley wore black silk stockings.

I don't go in for this outward show that one sees in the churches now. A lady said to me a few days ago, "Why,

118. Eugene de Sartiges (1809–92), a French diplomat, served as the minister plenipotentiary to the United States from 1850 until 1860. During his appointment, he lived for a time at Carolina Place. The house was next occupied by his successor, Edouard Henri Mercier, who served as French ambassador from July 1860 through December 1863. Jackson, *Chronicles of Georgetown, D.C.*, 32; and "From Washington," *New York Times*, p. 1. The *Evening Star* newspaper reported that the fire occurred on March 5, 1862.

119. Rev. John Thomson Brooke (1800–1861) was the rector of Christ Church Georgetown from 1824 to 1835. He was described in his obituary as "a strict Calvinist, he held very low views of the Ministry and Sacraments, and he maintained strong party affinities." This might explain his disdain for dancing and his refusal to confirm anyone who did not renounce it. See "Obituary Notices," *American Quarterly Church Review and Ecclesiastical Register*, vol. 14 (January 1862): 557. St. John's Episcopal Church, Georgetown, was closed for a period of eight years from 1831 to 1839. During this time, Britannia and her family attended Christ Church, located at the corner of 31st and O Streets in Georgetown. Sister America is America Pinckney Peter Williams (1803–42), Britannia's older sister. St. John's Episcopal Church, which opened in 1816, was designed by Benjamin Henry Latrobe and was located across Lafayette Square from the White House. Rev. William Dickinson Hawley (1784–1845) served as rector of St. John's Lafayette Square from 1817 to 1845.

120. Two renovations to the interior of St. John's Lafayette Square had occurred by the time Britannia recounted this information to her grandchildren in 1897. In 1842–43, the box and high-back pews were changed to low-back seats, the original brick paving of the floor was removed, the aisles were altered, the chancel was enlarged, and the original pulpit was replaced. A further renovation in 1883 replaced Latrobe's windows with stained glass windows, enlarged the chancel, and included an addition to the southeast corner of the church for a chantry, new vestry room, choir rooms, and offices. See Grimmett, *St. John's Church, Lafayette Square*, 23–25, 123.

121. John Laird (ca. 1767–1833), a Georgetown tobacco merchant, was the grandfather of William Laird Jr. In 1859 Thomas Bloomer Balch recalled old Mr. Laird as "singularly neat in his dress and very uniform in his habits." Balch, *Reminiscences of Georgetown*, 12. William Laird Jr. (1828–91), Britannia's first cousin once removed, was the son of William Laird Sr. and Helen Dunlop Laird.

Mrs. Kennon, if we did not have these things in the churches, the churches would be depopulated; the young people would not come!" To which I replied: "If that constitutes the religion of the young people of the present day I think they had better stay at home."

It was about Christmas time [1840 or 1850] and we were decorating St. John's Church, (Georgetown) I got up so early that frosty morning to gather the fresh box to sew on the little paste board cross I had made myself. Then, with the tacks and hammer, I went to St. John's Church and tacked it upon the pulpit. I was so pleased with my pretty cross as I believe was the Rev. Mr. Tillinghast;[122] but the next morning poor Mr. Tillinghast came to see me, <u>at the request of the congregation</u>, and asked me to take it down. He told me he had no objection to it and it was only in compliance with the request of the congregation that he requested its removal.

122. Rev. Nicholas Power Tillinghast (1817–69) served as rector of St. John's Georgetown from 1848 to 1867. A native of Providence, Rhode Island, he attended Brown University and the Virginia Theological Seminary. His previous appointments were at Monumental Church in Richmond, Virginia; a church in Society Hill, South Carolina; and Trinity Episcopal in Washington, where he served as interim rector.

The Rev. Dr. Register, who now has [St. Paul's Episcopal] Church in Buffalo, was in town some time ago and during his stay, kindly called to see us.[123] Before leaving he inquired after Freeland and I said to him:[124] "I hear Doctor that you are a warm advocate of the northern seminaries" (for he wanted Armistead, Dr. Peter, to send Freeland to the General Theological Seminary in New York as they pushed students more[125]), "now you were educated at the Seminary in Virginia!" He thanked me for the compliment and blushed up to his eyes. "There was Bishop Potter[126]— your own Bishop. He was educated at the same place! Philips Brooks, the last Bishop of Massachusetts, was also educated at the Virginia Seminary, and my only wish is that Freeland may imitate his good example."[127] Dr. Register could say nothing more.

123. Britannia first met Rev. Jacob Asbury Regester (1852–1916) when she traveled to Buffalo, New York, in August 1893 to visit the grave of her sister America. At the time of her visit, Register was the rector of St. Paul's Episcopal Church in Buffalo.

124. Rev. Dr. George Freeland Peter (1875–1953) was Britannia's youngest grandson, the son of Dr. Armistead Peter and Martha "Markie" Kennon Peter. He attended the General Theological Seminary in New York City and was ordained in 1899. In addition to serving churches in Washington, Richmond, Virginia, and Wheeling, West Virginia, he served as canon of Washington National Cathedral from 1928 to 1936.

125. Dr. Armistead Peter (1840–1902), Britannia's first cousin and son-in-law, was a son of Maj. George Peter and his third wife, Sarah Freeland Peter. He married Britannia's daughter, Martha "Markie" Kennon, in 1867.

126. Bishop Henry Codman Potter (1834–1908), the seventh bishop of the Episcopal Diocese of New York, graduated from the Virginia Theological Seminary in 1857.

127. Rev. Phillips Brooks (1825–93) was the longtime rector of Trinity Church, Boston, and lyricist of the popular hymn, "Oh, Little Town of Bethlehem." Brooks graduated from Virginia Theological Seminary in 1859.

was a collation served a great many people went who were not invited. In the course of the evening one of the guests asked her partner after the dance was over to request the band to play a march where upon everyone, supposing it was to announce supper, went to the state dining room which was not open. General Jackson had to come himself and speaking in a very peremptory way informed the company that supper was not ready.

Undated

Editorial note: The following five paragraphs originally appear in an undated document written by Britannia W. Kennon at the request of her grandson Armistead Peter Jr. When he compiled a portion of his grandmother's reminiscences, these paragraphs were included here.

In compliance with a request from my grandson, I am writing out a few memories of the old and most valued friends of my Father and Mother.[146] The Thornton family were frequent visitors at Tudor Place, especially on summer evenings, to the great pleasure of us all.[147] Their yellow carriage,

146. The grandson referred to here is Armistead Peter Jr., who frequently prompted his grandmother to recall the aspects of her earlier life and childhood and served as the primary secretary for recording these reminiscences.

147. Dr. William Thornton (1759–1828) and his wife, Anna Maria Brodeau Thornton (1775–1865), were close friends of Britannia's parents, Thomas and Martha Peter. Dr. Thornton was a physician and amateur architect who designed Tudor Place for Mr. and Mrs. Peter.

driven by George, was always hailed with delight.[148] After depositing its load, George would drive to the locust tree, still standing by the box circle, and await the time of departure.[149]

I was but a child of twelve years old when Dr. Thornton died but remember hearing him always spoken of as a man with great talent.[150] He was fond of the turf and had many engravings for fine horses of that day, together with a number of books on the same, all of which Mrs. Thornton gave to my father after his (the doctor's) death.[151]

They visited Mt. Vernon after their marriage and were presented by Genl Washington with a pair of Gerondoles, which have since been purchased by the Regents and are now at Mount Vernon.[152]

Mrs. Thornton was a highly talented woman, daughter of Mrs. Brodeau of Phila—I have heard my Mother say, she was sometimes called upon to translate for the Departments.[153]

Dr. Thornton intended on building a fine house in the norther part of Wash[ington]—the doors of which were to have been of birds-eye maple.

148. George was the Thornton's enslaved coachman.

149. A locust tree, *Gleditsia triacanthos*, in the boxwood circle north of the front doors of Tudor Place was where horses were tied. This tree was removed in the early twentieth century after it died, but a fragment of the stump remains.

150. William Thornton died March 28, 1828. *The National Intelligencer* newspaper of March 29, 1828, noted, "'Died: at his residence in F St, after a tedious confinement, by malady, Dr Wm Thornton, one of the oldest & most respectable inhabitants of Wash City. His funeral will take place on Sunday next."

151. Britannia's father Thomas Peter was also an authority on racehorses. Following Dr. Thornton's death, his widow consulted Peter regarding the possible sale of a horse. See Kail, "On the Track."

152. William Thornton married fifteen-year-old Anna Maria Brodeau on October 13, 1790. Britannia is referring to a pair of mahogany candlestands that Thornton actually purchased at the 1802 sale of Martha Washington's estate for $18. In 1887 the Mount Vernon Ladies' Association acquired the candlestands from Thornton's descendants, and they remain in Mount Vernon's collection as accession numbers W-1a and W-1b. "Martha Washington Estate Sale List in hand of Thomas Peter," 1802, TPA.

153. Mrs. Thornton's mother, Ann Brodeau (?–1836), was born in England but immigrated with her daughter to Philadelphia in 1780, where she operated a boarding school for young ladies that was located on Lodge Alley. She died in Washington in 1836 and was buried in Congressional Cemetery.

I often think now how different it all is from what it was in those good old days. These people lived for the most part <u>within</u> <u>themselves</u>! We raised our own beef, mutton, poultry—and fine fowls we had and had our own dairy where the butter was made. Then there was the garden where the vegetables were raised— the orchard from which we had an abundance of fine fruit. The fruit was put up for Winter use, either preserved, canned or dried; vegetables were stored away and herbs were dried (for where was there a place in those days without its herb garden!) for seasoning.

The wool was sheared from the sheep— washed, carded, dyed, spun and woven into linseys, either striped or in plaids, for the women's dresses or dyed plain and sent to the fulling mill to be fulled for the men's clothing.[186] Flax was grown and woven for domestic use.[187] The fine linen was imported, of course.[188] On the plantations there were among the slaves, shoemakers, carpenters, blacksmiths, weavers, etc. They were <u>trained</u> for those purposes. It was worth one's while to train a servant in those days

186. Carding was the process of detangling, cleaning, and intermixing wool fibers to produce a continuous strand of wool thread. Prior to mechanization during the nineteenth century, carding was done by hand using two rectangular wooden cards with metal teeth. Linsey, also known as linsey-woolsey, was a coarse cloth made from a linen warp and a woolen weft. Montgomery, *Textiles in America*, 279. A fulling mill was a mill were wool was processed by mechanization. In woolen cloth production, fulling is the step that involves cleaning the wool to eliminate dirt, oil, and other impurities, which also makes it thicker.

187. Flax, *Linum usitatissimum*, is a fibrous crop whose stalks can be processed into linen that can be used for textiles.

188. In the early nineteenth century, linen imported to the United States typically came from England, Scotland, and Ireland. Most was produced in the British Isles, but other linen was European in origin and imported into London. See Harte, "British Linen Trade."

and great pain was often taken to have them proficient in their different occupations. The cook was the autocrat of the kitchen and woe betide the luckless kitchen girl who dared to disobey her orders. When she became too old to cook one of the younger women, who had been under her, maybe from childhood, was ready to take her place and the "servant question" had no terrors for the mistress in those days.[189]

The same applied to the house servants. I remember hearing my father tell the following story.[190] The old dining room servant at his father's home had a granddaughter, a young girl who always assisted him at the table.[191] On the occasion a gentleman who was staying at the house dining with them told a very funny story. Old ———'s face never cracked a smile but not so with the girl.[192] She broke out into a loud ha! The old man gave her a look and commenced to edge toward her gradually until she left the room whence he followed her.

189. In the late nineteenth century, the "servant question" referred to the common problem of finding and retaining good domestic servants as well as a demand for good servants that outweighed the available supply. Periodicals such as *Good Housekeeping* and *Cosmopolitan* frequently included articles on the subject. See Katzman, *Seven Days a Week*, 358.

190. Britannia's father was Thomas Peter (1769–1834).

191. Thomas Peter's father and Britannia's grandfather was Robert Peter (1726–1806).

192. This servant's name is omitted in all manuscript and typescript versions of Britannia Kennon's Reminiscences compiled by Armistead Peter Jr..

Decoration Day was not begun by the Northerners, as is usually supposed, but by the Southerners and afterwards copied by the North.[193] I remember the first Decoration Day at Arlington.[194] It seems that an order was issued prohibiting any of the southern graves at "Arlington" being decorated on that day. It just showed the vindictive spirit of the North! I said, if that was the case, not a flower should go from "Tudor" to "Arlington" on that day. In the morning several came to beg flowers but I refused to give them. Later in the day the servant came in and said a man was at the door who wanted some flowers. I sent word that I had none to give to go to "Arlington." He then sent in his name and an apology for coming. I went to the door and found it was Powell, Dr. Sutherland's old orderly.[195] He apologized for coming, saying that the flowers were not for general decoration but to be placed on his brother's grave who was buried there. I then told him my reason for declining his request in the first place, but, as they were for his brother's

193. Following the Civil War, Decoration Day was an occasion where the graves of Civil War casualties were decorated with flowers. It is now the holiday known as Memorial Day, which honors all military personnel who died while serving in the United States armed forces. Southern Memorial Day or Decoration Day was first observed by a group of ladies in Columbus, Georgia, on April 25, 1866, when they laid flowers on the graves of both Union and Confederate dead. See Coulter, *South during Reconstruction*, 178–79.

194. The first national observation of Decoration Day took place on May 30, 1868, as proclaimed by the Grand Army of the Republic, the organization for Union Army veterans. A ceremony was held at Arlington Cemetery after which five thousand participants decorated the graves of more than twenty thousand Civil War dead buried there.

195. This is possibly Dr. William P. Powell (1834–1915). In 1863 he was hired as a contract assistant surgeon for the Union Army and later worked for a year at the Contraband Hospital, a facility in Washington providing medical care to former slaves. Dr. Charles Sutherland (1831–95) was a Union Army doctor and hospital administrator. In the spring of 1864 he was appointed medical purveyor for the Army of the Potomac, where he supervised twenty hospitals in and around Washington, DC. He later served as surgeon general of the US Army from 1891 to 1893.

grave, who, by the way, was a Union soldier—he should have them. I went to the garden and picked him a large bunch which he was loth to accept, but I insisted that he should. The joke of it was, that evening, as is often the case, a high wind storm came up and blew the flowers off the Union graves and on to the graves of the Confederates.

December 14, 1900

The old flower knot was laid out in triangles and odd shaped beds—an oval bed in the center with a beautiful laburnum in the middle.[196] These beds were each surrounded by a low box hedge, with paths in between. One bed was always planted with lavender, of which father was so fond. Mother would dry it and put it into little bags; these, she would lay between the linen in the closet and the whole place would be perfumed. The other beds had butter and eggs, jonquils, daffodils, Canterbury bells, larkspur (double and single), lilies of the valley (my favorites), wallflowers—of which mother was so fond—sweet Williams,

196. In this passage, Britannia discusses a landscape feature in the Tudor Place garden composed of multiple triangular flowerbeds bordered by bushes of English boxwood. During Britannia's absence from Tudor Place between 1858 and 1861, the original box knot was largely destroyed when the box was cut and used for holiday greenery by neighbors. Jane Johns Peter Beverly, niece of Thomas and Martha Peter, was a frequent visitor to the Tudor Place garden, and she later reproduced the design of the Tudor Place box knot in the garden at her Virginia estate, Avenel. The design of the Avenel box knot was published in Edith Tunis Sale's *Historic Gardens of Virginia* (1923), allowing Armistead Peter 3rd, Britannia's great-grandson and a later owner of Tudor Place, to replant the Tudor Place box knot in 1933. The new box knot was placed on the opposite side of the center walk in order to preserve the few remaining box bushes that survived from the original nineteenth-century landscape feature. The present box knot at Tudor Place, on the location of the 1929 version, was planted in 2012 following an extensive archaeological survey of this portion of the garden. Laburnum is commonly known as "golden rain," *Laburnum anagyroides.*

roses, yellow lilies and many other kinds of old-fashioned flowers.[197]

I never see the sweet old monthly honeysuckle now! It was something like a wild honeysuckle but a vine, not a bush, and so sweet. Then, there used to be quantities of coral honeysuckle.[198] When I returned to the dear old place, after renting it to the Pendletons, the flower knot was grown up in weeds, the box untrimmed and grown to such a size.[199] In fact, the whole place was neglected and unkempt! I had the box moved and planted about the place. That down by the arbor lived but the rest died in spite of the care I took in moving it. Those round boxbushes are the corners of the beds in the old flower knot.[200] The tree box, by the serviceberry, Mother planted.[201]

November 22, 1900

Mason's Ferry.[202] The old ferry across the Potomac in my young days consisted of a scow or "team boat" as it was called. A flatboat, with two large, round stones on either side of the boat. A stall was built about each of these stones consisting of posts,

197. "Butter and eggs," also known as yellow toadflax, *Linaria vulgaris*; jonquils, *Narcissus jonquilla*; daffodils, *Narcissus, sp.*; "Canterbury bells," also known as bellflower, *Campanula medium*; larkspur, *Consolida regalis*; lily of the valley, *Convallaria majalis*; wallflowers, *Erysimum sp.*; sweet Williams, *Dianthus barbatus*; and yellow lilies, *Lilium canadense*. A variety of roses were planted in the Tudor Place garden. Britannia Kennon's grandson Armistead Peter Jr., the owner of Tudor Place from 1911 to 1960, as well as her great-grandson, Armistead Peter 3rd, owner of Tudor Place from 1960 to 1983, both reintroduced many of the heirloom varieties of roses that had been found in the Tudor Place garden in the early nineteenth century during their respective periods of ownership.

198. *Lonicera sempervirens* is a species of honeysuckle native to the eastern United States.

199. Britannia Kennon returned to Tudor Place on January 1, 1862. William Armistead Pendleton and family leased Tudor Place from Britannia from 1858 to 1861; see note 57. "Box" refers to boxwood, much of it planted at the time the house was completed in 1816. The boxwood circle located in front of the north facade of Tudor Place is one of these ca. 1816 original features still remaining in the Tudor Place garden.

200. See note 196.

201. Serviceberry, *Amelanchier*.

202. John Mason (1766–1849), the son of George Mason of Gunston Hall, owned a ferry that provided service from Georgetown across the Potomac River to the Virginia shore. Prior to the completion of the carriageway on the Aqueduct Bridge in 1843, which featured a narrow roadway, the ferry was the only way to cross the Potomac at Georgetown.

with a roof, or covering, over them. In each of the stalls stood a horse. These stones revolved 'round and 'round by the constant treading of the horses and the boat was thereby propelled across the river. It was said that eventually the horses would go blind by constant treading!

Yes, I've crossed on it many times in the carriage when driving to "Arlington."[203] It was the only way we had of crossing the river in those days! Mr. Mason also kept a rowboard for his guests to cross to the island in.[204] The steamboat went from Water street—about the foot of High Street—and landed on the Virginia side just above the old causeway.[205]

May 11, 1900

Ann G. Wightt took the name of Sister Gertrude when she entered the convent.[206] "Sister Getty," the girls called her. She was placed at the convent when a child. Her parents died and feeling alone in the world she decided at the age of fifteen to take the veil and become a nun. She

203. Arlington, the Virginia plantation of Britannia's uncle George Washington Parke Custis. The property was part of a 1,100-acre tract originally purchased by Cutis's father, John Parke Custis, in 1778. G.W.P. Custis inherited the property after his father's death, naming it Arlington after the ancestral Custis family estate on the eastern shore of Virginia. Custis owned the property until his death in 1857, at which time it was inherited by his daughter, Mary Custis Lee, for her lifetime, after which it would pass to Custis's eldest grandson, George Washington Custis Lee. However, Arlington was seized by the Union Army in May of 1861 and later purchased by the federal government after the Lees were unable to pay taxes on the property. The first burials on the property occurred in 1864, and today the mansion is surrounded by more than six hundred acres of Arlington National Cemetery.

204. John Mason, see note 202, also owned Analostan Island, located just off of the Virginia shore, where he kept a summer residence. John Mason sold the island in 1833; after subsequent owners, this island became known by its present name of the Theodore Roosevelt Island National Memorial. For a cultural history of the island, see Historic American Landscape Survey, Theodore Roosevelt Island, HALS No. DC-12 (Washington, DC: National Park Service, US Department of the Interior, n.d.).

205. Water Street is present-day K Street in Georgetown. High Street is now Wisconsin Avenue, the major north–south thoroughfare in Georgetown. See appendix 1 for Georgetown street names prior to 1895. In 1807 the Georgetown Common Council authorized, at public expense, the construction of a causeway from the Virginia shore to the northwest corner of Mason's island. The 380-foot-long causeway was intended to divert the flow of the Potomac River because alluvial deposits between the island and the port of Georgetown hindered river navigation. The ferry landing was located adjacent to the causeway.

206. Ann Gertrude Wightt (1799–1867), later Sister Gertrude, was the daughter of a prominent Catholic slaveholding family of Maryland. Following the deaths of both parents, she was placed in Georgetown Visitation Convent's Young Ladies Academy, where she remained for six years. Following the completion of her education in 1814, she entered the convent as a novitiate. As an instructor, students, including Britannia, called her "Sister Getty." Over the next decade Sister Gertrude assumed several prominent leadership posts and was appointed directress of the academy in 1826. An appointment as assistant superior followed, and then she abruptly left the cloister on the afternoon of March 21, 1831, and never returned. For a full biography of Wightt, see Mannard, "To Raise the Academy." The Monastery of the Visitation,

remained at the convent for fifteen years, being at the head of the school while I was a pupil there and still holding that position when she left.[207] Feeling that it was not her vocation she determined to leave and without saying anything to any one about her determination, she put on one of the boarder's (the girls being in class at the time) long cloaks and bonnet, which completely covered her habit; opened the door and walked out.[208] On reaching the street she hardly knew which way to go but walked along until she reached the Union Hotel.[209] On her way she was met by a Catholic priest who thought there was something in her face that he recognized, yet could not satisfy himself that it could be her. He went directly to the monastery, rung the bell and inquired for her.[210] It was the first intimation the sisters had that she had left. At the hotel she took a carriage and told the man to drive her to General Van Nesses'.[211] He didn't know the way but she (without revealing her identity) told him to inquire along the route, which he did, until they found the place. On arriving she inquired of the servant

Georgetown, was founded in 1798–99 as a monastery of the Visitation Order by Sister Teresa Lalor, VHM (ca. 1769–1846), and the Most Reverend Leonard Neale, SJ (1746–1817), who was then serving as president of Georgetown College. See Sullivan, *Georgetown Visitation since 1799*, for a complete history of the monastery.

207. Britannia attended the school for four years starting in the late 1820s when it was known as The Young Ladies Academy of the Visitation.

208. The likely reason for Sister Gertrude's 1831 departure is that it followed a failed "coup" in which she, with the support of Father Lopez, proposed to change the rule of the Georgetown Convent from the Visitation Order to the Ursuline Order. See Mannard, "To Raise the Academy." For a similar though slightly varying account of Sister Gertrude's escape from the one presented by Britannia, see Gouverneur, *As I Remember*, 224. See also "She Left a Convent," *Evening Star*, March 29, 1892, p. 8.

209. The Union Hotel was located at the corner of M and 30th Streets in Georgetown. See note 31.

210. That is, the Monastery of the Visitation, Georgetown. See note 206.

211. Maj. Gen. John P. Van Ness (1769–1846) and his wife, Marcia Burnes Van Ness (1782–1832), lived on a property bounded by what is now C Street, Constitution Avenue, 17th Street and 18th Street. The Van Ness house was designed by Benjamin Henry Latrobe and constructed between 1813 and 1816; the house was demolished in 1908.

whether Mrs. Van Ness was at home, which she said she was, but was very much engaged and could not see callers—being occupied by a dinner. She told the servant that she was a cousin of Mrs. Van Nesses' and said: "you can just show me to her room."[212] After the dinner was over Mrs. Van Ness went to see her and you can imagine her surprise at finding Miss Wightt. They sent a note to the convent telling them that she was there. The priests went down there and implored her to return but she wouldn't hear of it. Madam Iturbide, who, at that time, was residing in Georgetown, invited her to come to her house and teach her two daughters, which she did for a year or more.[213] Her hair was cut short while a sister and she wore a muslin cap—which prevented her from going out in society. Mrs. Van Ness, her cousin, begged that she would come and make her house her permanent home, which she did; remaining there until after General Van Ness died.[214] Mrs. Van Ness had one daughter, Ann, who married Mr. Arthur Middleton, of South Carolina, but died in childbirth before Miss Wightt went there.[215] I don't know

212. Wightt was the first cousin of Mrs. Van Ness. Her father, John Wightt, was the brother of Ann Wightt Burnes, Marcia Burnes Van Ness's mother.

213. Ana María de Huarte y Muñiz Iturbide (1786–1861) was the queen consort of Emperor Augustin I of Mexico, whom she married in 1805. Emperor Augustin I of Mexico reigned from May 1822 until his abdication in March 1823. During her husband's reign, she was styled "Her Imperial Majesty Empress Ana Maria of Mexico." Following the emperor's abdication and subsequent execution, the former empress, her children, a chaplain, and a dozen attendants sailed to New Orleans in September 1824. From New Orleans the group traveled up the Mississippi and Ohio Rivers via steamboat to Wheeling, West Virginia, then traveled overland to Baltimore and south to Georgetown. One of Iturbide's daughters, Juana María de Iturbide (1812–28), was a novice at the Convent of the Visitation in Georgetown. On her deathbed she professed herself a nun and took the name Sister Margarita of Jesus, Marie, and Joseph. She was buried in the crypt of the convent chapel following her 1828 death.

214. Maj. Gen. John P. Van Ness (1769–1846) died on March 7, 1846. Major General Van Ness came to Washington as a representative from New York, serving from 1801 until 1803, at which time he accepted President Thomas Jefferson's appointment to be the major of the militia of the District of Columbia. He was promoted to lieutenant colonel in 1805, brigadier general in 1811, and major general in 1813. From 1830 to 1834, he served as mayor of Washington, DC.

215. Ann Elbertina Van Ness Middleton (1803–23) was the only child of Major General and Mrs. Van Ness. She married Arthur Middleton (1795–1853), the eldest son of South Carolina governor Henry Middleton and the grandson and namesake of Arthur Middleton, one of the South Carolina signers of the Declaration of Independence, in 1823. A day after giving birth to their daughter, Marcia Helen Middleton, both Ann and the baby died on November 22, 1823, when she contracted a malignant fever following childbirth. Both Ann and her infant daughter were later interred in a large neoclassical mausoleum constructed by General Van Ness on the south side of H Street NW between 9th and 10th Streets. The mausoleum was later moved to Oak Hill Cemetery in 1874, where it is located today.

and borrowed them for him.[249] After copying them Cousin Mary carelessly put them in a drawer and there they remained, being tumbled about with other papers until Mother sent to "Arlington" for them.[250] The letter dated "Philadelphia, June 18, 1775" was so badly torn that mother said it should never go out of her possession again.[251]

Edmond Law Rogers repaired it as best he could, adding at the time the following inscription:[252] "This letter was repaired for Mrs. Martha Peter by her great nephew, Edmond Law Rogers, Tudor Place Georgetown, and Grandson of her sister Eliza Parke Custis. A facsimile was taken by him before repairing the letter. Edmond Law Rogers, Feb 1st 1849."

Armistead Peter Jr. Note: In speaking of this letter, Lossing says it "is carefully preserved at Arlington House by her great grand-daughter Mrs. Mary Custis Lee."[253] This is an erroneous statement, though to whom the blame should be attached I cannot say. The letter is also copied in "Custis Recollections" but very imperfectly as will be seen by a comparison to the text.... Grandmother gave me this letter on my 30th birthday, Nov 30, 1900.[254]

249. Jared Sparks (1789–1866) was a historian, author, and later president of Harvard University. Sparks was given access to President Washington's papers and edited a twelve-volume compilation of the correspondence that was published between 1834 and 1837 as *The Writings of George Washington*. Sparks first visited Tudor Place in 1828 while conducting research for an earlier book. In 1839 Sparks published a separate work, *The Life of George Washington; to which Are Added His Diaries and Speeches; and Various Miscellaneous Papers Relating to His Habits and Opinions*. Uncle Custis is George Washington Parke Custis (1781–1857), Britannia's uncle. Mother is Martha Custis Peter.

250. Cousin Mary is Mary Anna Randolph Custis Lee (1807–73), Britannia's first cousin, the wife of Robert E. Lee and the daughter of George Washington Parke Custis.

251. This June 18, 1775, letter from George Washington to Martha Washington, written from Philadelphia, informed her that he was given command of the Continental Army. The letter was found by Martha Peter in the drawer of the writing desk she inherited from Martha Washington. A transcription of the letter is found on the following page. Britannia gave the June 18, 1775, letter to her grandson Armistead Peter Jr. on the occasion of his thirtieth birthday in 1900. It was later inherited by his son, Armistead Peter 3rd, and remains in the Tudor Place collection.

252. Edmond Law Rogers (1818–96) was Britannia's first cousin once removed. Rogers was the grandson of Eliza Custis Law, and he owned a sizable collection of Washington objects inherited from both his mother and grandmother.

253. Benson John Lossing (1813–91) was an American historian and author of more than forty books focused on American history. In 1859 Lossing published *Mount Vernon and Its Associations*, the work Britannia is discussing in this paragraph.

254. In 1860 Britannia's cousin Mary Anna Custis Lee (1807–73) published *Recollections and Private Memoirs of Washington by His Adopted Son, George Washington Parke Custis, with a Memoir of the Author by His Daughter*. Lee began the project in 1857, a few years before her father's death, editing a collection of articles he wrote for the *National Intelligencer* about his childhood spent with George and Martha Washington.

Philadelphia June 18, 1775

Editorial Note: In all compilations of
Britannia Kennon's Reminiscences anthologized by her grandson Armistead Peter Jr.,
he included a full transcription of this June
18, 1775, letter from George Washington to
Martha Washington, then in his possession
and now in the Tudor Place Archives.

My Dearest,

    I am now set down to write you on
a subject which fills me with inex-
pressible concern—and this concern is
greatly aggravated and Increased, when
I reflect upon the uneasiness I know it
will give you—It has been determined
in Congress that the whole Army raised
for the defence of the American Cause
shall be put under my care, and that it
is necessary for me to proceed immediately to Boston to take upon me the
command of it. You may believe me my
dear Patcy, when I assure you, in the
most solemn manner, that, so far from
seeking this appointment I have used
every endeavor in my power to avoid
it, not only from my unwillingness to
part with you and the Family, but from
a consciousness of its being a trust too
great for my Capacity and that I should

enjoy more real happiness and felicity in one month with you, at home, than I have the most distant prospect of reaping abroad, if my stay were to be Seven times Seven years. But, as it has been a kind of destiny that has thrown me upon this Service, I shall hope that my undertaking of it, is designed to answer some good purpose—You might, and I suppose did perceive, from the Tenor of my letters, that I was apprehensive I could not avoid this appointment, as I did not even pretend [t]o intimate when I should return—that was the case—it was utterly out of my power to refuse this appointment without exposing my Character to such censures as would have reflected dishonour upon myself, and given pain to my friends— this, I am sure could not, and ought not be pleasing to you, & must have lessened me considerably in my own esteem. I shall rely therefore, confidently, on that Providence which has heretofore preservd, & been bountiful to me, not doubting but that I shall return safe to you in the fall—I shall feel no pain from the Toil, or the danger of the Campaign—My unhapiness will flow, from the uneasiness I know you will feel at being left alone—I beg of

you to summon your whole fortitude
Resolution, and pass your time as agree-
ably as possible—nothing will give me
so much sincere satisfaction as to hear
this, and to hear it from your own pen.

If it should be your desire to remove
to Alexandria (as you once mentioned
upon an occasion of this sort) I am
quite pleased that you should put it
into practice, & Lund Washington[255]
may be directed, by you, to build
a Kitchen and other Houses there
proper for your reception—if on the
other hand you should rather Incline
to spend a good part of your time
among your Friends below, I wish you
to do so.—In short, my earnest, &
ardent desire is, that you would pursue
any Plan that is most likely to produce
content, and a tolerable degree of
Tranquility as it must add greatly to
my uneasy feelings to hear that you are
dissatisfied, and complaining at what I
really could not avoid.

As life is always uncertain, and
common prudence dictates to every Man the necessity of settling his
temporal Concerns whilst it is in his
power—and while the Mind is calm
and undisturbed, I have, since I came
to this place (for I had not time to do it

255. Lund Washington (1737–96), George Washington's distant cousin, served as a steward of Mount Vernon during the time that Washington was away commanding the Continental Army.

before I left home) got Colo Pendleton to Draft a Will for me by the directions which I gave him which will I now Inclose—The Provision made for you, in cas[e] of my death will, I hope, be agreeable; I Included the money for which I sold my own land (to Doctr Mercer [256]) in the Sum Given you, as also all other Debts. What I owe myself is very trifling—Cary's Debt excepted, and that would not have been much if the Bank stock had been applied without such difficulties as he made in the Transference.[257]

I shall add nothing more at present as I have several Letters to write, but to desire you will remember me to Milly[258] & all Friends, and to assure you that I am with the most unfeigned regard,

My dear
Patcy Yr Affecte
Gº: Washington

P.S. Since writing the above I have receivd your Letter of the 15th and have got two suits of what I was told wa[s] the prettiest Muslin.[259] I wish it may please you—it cost 50/ a suit that is 20/ a yard.

256. Dr. Hugh F. Mercer (1726–77), brigadier general in the Continental Army and close friend of Washington, died in 1777 from wounds received during the Battle of Princeton.

257. In June of 1774 Washington directed Robert Cary & Company of London to sell Bank of England stock from the estate of his stepdaughter Martha "Patsy" Parke Custis, who died the previous year, and to use the proceeds to pay off the debt he owed their firm for the importation of goods from England to Virginia. In the spring of 1775, shortly before he departed for Philadelphia, he learned that the documents he submitted were unacceptable to the bank's directors and that new documents would need to be executed. He didn't resolve the matter until after the end of the war. See Abbot, *Papers of George Washington, Revolutionary War Series*, 1:3–6n7.

258. Amelia "Milly" Posey (ca. 1762–?), daughter of George Washington's former neighbor Capt. John Posey, had been a friend and playmate of Martha Washington's daughter Martha "Patsy" Parke Custis (1756–73). Milly Posey lived at Mount Vernon for much of the American Revolution. Posey, *General Thomas Posey*, 281.

259. Muslin is a lightweight, plainly woven cotton fabric used for clothing and household textiles. Prior to the invention of the mule-jenny in 1779, most muslins were imported from India. However this invention made the manufacture of fine cotton yarns possible, so muslins could be spun in England and Scotland. Montgomery, *Textiles in America*, 304.

Phil.d June 23, 1775

Editorial Note: In his later compilation of Britannia's reminiscences, Armistead Peter Jr. also included a full transcription of the June 23, 1775, letter from George Washington to Martha Washington that was also owned by his grandmother until her death in 1911. This letter was inherited by Britannia's grandson G. Freeland Peter, and it later returned to Mount Vernon following his death.

My dearest,

As I am within a few Minutes of leaving this City,[260] I could not think of departing from it without dropping you a line; especially as I do not know whether it may be in my power to write again till I get to the Camp at Boston—I go fully trusting in that Providence, which has been more bountiful to me than I deserve, & in full confidence of a happy meeting with you sometime in the Fall—I have not time to add more, as I am surrounded with Company to take leave of me—I retain an unalterable affection for you, which neither time or distance can change, my best love to Jack & Nelly,[261] & regard for the

260. This letter was written from Philadelphia just prior to Washington's departure for Boston.

261. John "Jack" Parke Custis (1754–81), Martha Washington's son from her first marriage to Daniel Parke Custis; and Eleanor "Nelly" Calvert Custis (1754/1757/1758–1811), Martha Washington's daughter-in-law. Eleanor married John on February 3, 1774.

rest of the Family concludes me with the utmost truth & sincerety Yr entire Gº: Washington

[Address] To Mrs. Washington at Mount Vernon

<hr />

Family Notes of Interest from Grandmother and a Few Notes from Other Sources Compiled by Armistead Peter Jr. of Georgetown, DC.

April 6, 1895

When your Grandfather, Captain Kennon was in command of the Washington Navy Yard, he called at "Tudor Place" one afternoon with Mrs. Clark (daughter of Mr. Robert Beverly of "Blandfield," Virginia[262]) but I was not at home.[263] Shortly after that, Miss Ann Tayloe (daughter of [Colonel John Tayloe]) was married at the "Octagon" to Henry Lewis.[264] The next week a reception was given at the "Octagon" to which we were invited. As Mrs. Clark had no carriage, Mother asked her to go with us,

262. Robert Beverley (1769–1843), son of Robert Beverley (1740–1800) and Maria Carter Beverley (1745–1817). In 1805 Robert Beverley purchased the property across R Street from Tudor Place, naming the estate Acrolophos. Blandfield was the Essex County, Virginia, plantation of the Beverley family. The house was constructed between 1716 and 1720 for William Beverley, and the estate descended in the Beverley family for subsequent generations, including those described here by Britannia.

263. Beverley Kennon (1793–1844) and Britannia married on December 8, 1842. Maria Beverley Clarke (1791–aft. 1860) was the daughter of Robert Beverley, who owned Acrolophos (now Dumbarton Oaks) across R Street from Tudor Place. Maria married Dr. George Clarke (1789–1822) of Georgetown and was widowed after he died of typhoid fever in 1822. Maria was the second cousin of Beverley Kennon, who through his mother was a descendant of the Beverley family of Blandfield.

264. Ann Ogle Tayloe (1814–76), daughter of Colonel and Mrs. John Tayloe, married Henry Howell Lewis (1817–93) at her parents' home, the Octagon, on November 30, 1840.

and it was <u>there</u> I first met Captain Kennon.[265]

This reception was held on November 30—Your [Armistead Peter Jr.'s] birthday.

January 16, 1897

While your grandfather Kennon held the rank of Post Captain, he was entitled by courtesy to be called Commodore, having been in command of the Washington Navy Yard.[266] Post Captain was at that time the highest rank in the Navy but the commander of a yard, or of a squadron, was entitled by courtesy to be called Commodore.

April 4, 1895

When Mother and her elder sister were young ladies, they each wanted a watch and General Washington imported two watches for them at their request.[267] The faces, instead of being numbered by figures, were marked by their names, each of which had twelve letters—"Eliza P. Custis" and "Martha Custis."[268]

265. Britannia is describing the first time she met her future husband, Cdre. Beverley Kennon at a reception held at the Tayloes' home, the Octagon House, celebrating the marriage of their daughter Anne the previous week. Both Mrs. Clarke and Cdre. Beverley Kennon were distant cousins of the bride, Ann Ogle Tayloe, whose mother was also a member of the Beverley family of Virginia.

266. Beverley Kennon served as commandant of the Washington Navy Yard from April 27, 1841, to March 7, 1843. Hibben, *Navy-Yard, Washington*, 19. In the US Navy during the nineteenth century, the rank of commodore was typically used as a courtesy title reserved for captains in command of a fleet or squadron. Historically, the rank of commodore was not a higher rank but rather a temporary assignment. In 1899 the US Navy abolished the rank and did not use it again until World War II.

267. Martha Custis Peter (1777–1854), Britannia's mother, and Elizabeth "Eliza" Custis Law (1776–1831), Britannia's aunt.

268. The watch formerly belonging to Martha Custis is now in the collection of Washington's Headquarters State Historic Site in Newburg, New York. The watch was previously thought to belong to Martha Washington, but research by Elyse Zorn Karlin and Yvonne Markowitz determined that it belonged to Martha Custis Peter of Tudor Place. See Karlin and Markowitz, "Story behind the Martha Custis Pocket Watch."

battle was fought, on the road that leads to "Riversdale"—the graves have been filled in with red clay in which no grass would grow.[286]

286. Bladensburg, located in southwestern Maryland a few miles from the District of Columbia boundary line, was the site of the August 24, 1814, battle where British regulars and Royal Marines defeated American forces and then marched on Washington, DC. Riversdale was the home of George Calvert and his wife, Rosalie Stier Calvert, located in Prince George's County, Maryland. The Calverts were the uncle and aunt of Martha Custis Peter.

November 3, 1895

In 1813, Father and Mother with Brother Washington, who was then thirteen years old, drove to Philadelphia in their family carriage to visit Sister Columbia, who was at Madam Revardie's school.[287] It took four days to make the journey from Georgetown to Philadelphia in those days. On their return, Mother brought back some small flowers and plants for the greenhouse and among them was the Sago Palm which is still at "Tudor Place."[288]

287. Brother Washington is George Washington Peter (1801–77), Britannia's older brother. Columbia Washington Peter (1797–1820) was educated at Madame Rivardi's Seminary in Philadelphia starting in 1811. Her aunt Nelly Custis Lewis wrote to Elizabeth Bordley Gibson in Philadelphia on August 25, 1811, asking, "Will you permit me to encroach upon your kindness by asking your kind countenance for my Dear Niece & Godchild Columbia Washington Peter. My sister has determined to send her to Mrs. Rivardi's School in a month or two. She will be entirely a stranger in Philadelphia, and has always been so much with her Mother, that she will feel very lonely for some time." Brady, *George Washington's Beautiful Nelly*, 69–70. For more information on Rivardi's school, see Johnson, "Madame Rivardi's Seminary in the Gothic Mansion." Madame Rivardi's Seminary was located on Philadelphia's fashionable Chestnut Street. For biographical information on headmistress Maria von Born Rivardi, see Singerton, "United States as 'An Abode of Misery.'"

288. As Britannia describes, Thomas and Martha Peter purchased a sago palm, *Cycas revoluta*, in Philadelphia, which they brought back to Tudor Place. While this original sago palm was still living at the time Britannia W. Kennon gave these recollections, it died in the early twentieth century, although its third-generation descendants still remain at Tudor Place.

December 19, 1899

Mother was present at the laying of the cornerstone of the Capitol.[289] Yes, I have often heard her tell of it! She was a girl at the time and drove up from Hope Park where she lived, with other members of the family.[290] There was an ox killed and barbecued on the occasion, and after the cornerstone was put in place by General Washington and the speeches were made, everyone went and partook of the repast. Of course, they did not go being but girls but the General came to them (Mother said) and told them they must have something before they left and escorted them to the table. I have often heard her tell of it.

Armistead Peter Jr.: The cornerstone was laid Sept. 18 1793.

289. Martha Custis Peter, Britannia's mother, attended the laying of the Capitol cornerstone, which took place on September 18, 1793. The cornerstone was laid by President Washington and Masonic Grand Master Joseph Clark of Maryland in a full Masonic ceremony.

290. Hope Park was the Fairfax County estate of Dr. David Stuart, Martha Peter's stepfather. Located five miles north of Fairfax Courthouse, Stuart purchased the property in 1785.

[The family] spent the summers at Oakland.[291] The house was so small and I often think now how when we left there later in the fall and came down to Tudor what a change it was to come from that house, so simple, to this large house. Father kept his hounds as did Uncle George later.[292] When brother John bought Montevideo, he also kept hounds and they would put them together in the fall and go on a fox hunt.[293] Mother used to go too with Father and Cousin Henry Dunlop would come up and stay with us.[294] In the evening, after the days hunt, we would sit around the fire and they would sing hunting songs, tell stories, roast apples, and play "Hull-gull, [hands full, parcel], how many," with chestnuts.[295] Those were happy days. No formality, no ostentation, just happy days.

Armistead Peter Jr. Note: January 16, 1897, In speaking of Suter's Tavern, Georgetown, Grandmother says she can neither place its location nor remember anything concerning it and thinks that it passed out of existence long before her day.[296]

291. Oakland was Thomas and Martha Peter's Montgomery County, Maryland, estate. See note 185. The house at Oakland was probably typical of vernacular dwellings that were found in Montgomery County in the late eighteenth and early nineteenth century: a low frame structure of several rooms with a sharply pitched roof that also covered a narrow porch. A kitchen, springhouse, and other support structures were usually nearby with barns and dwellings for enslaved laborers on the property as well. See Kail, "Oakland," 3.

292. Thomas Peter (1769–1834), Britannia's father; and Maj. George Peter (1779–1861), Britannia's uncle.

293. John Parke Custis Peter (1799–1848), Britannia's brother, resided at Montevideo, an estate in Montgomery County, Maryland. It was formed from land inherited by Thomas Peter from his father, Robert Peter.

294. Henry Dunlop (1799–1877), Britannia's cousin, was the son of Elizabeth Peter Dunlop and James Dunlop.

295. Hull-gull was a children's game in which one player guesses how many small objects are in another player's hand and gives up or receives objects according to whether the guess is high, low, or exact.

296. John Suter (d. 1794) established a tavern in Georgetown in 1783 that was located near the intersection of 31st and K Streets. The tavern was the location for several meetings between George Washington, Pierre Charles L'Enfant, and Andrew Ellicott to discuss the surveying of the planned federal city.

The leading hotel in Georgetown in my earliest recollection was the Union Hotel.[297] Every morning the old stage, called the "Royal George" would be driven up to the hotel and take the members of Congress to the Capitol.[298] At that time there was only a dirt road (now Penn. Ave.) from Georgetown to the Capitol, and at times, a very rough and muddy road it was.[299]

April 28, 1897

Mother said that when they were children, their portraits were taken by Pine (I think) at "Mount Vernon."[300] After Grandmama's death, all of the pictures were left to Uncle Custis.[301] Aunt Lewis took hers, but what has become of it, I do not know.[302] Mother's, and a portrait of Aunt Patty Custis, the elder sister of John Parke Custis and daughter of Mrs. Washington, were here for years.[303] I knew that these pictures belonged to Uncle Custis, for Mother had often told me that she wished I might have the portrait of herself; for it was a happy little face, and on one occasion I know she asked Uncle Custis for it

297. The Union Hotel was located at the corner of Bridge Street and 30th Street in Georgetown. See note 31.

298. The Royal George was a stagecoach line that ran from Georgetown to Capitol Hill along Pennsylvania Avenue. Pulled by a team of four horses, the coach featured additional seats on the roof. Benjamin Henry Latrobe recalled that the Royal George "either rattled with members of Congress from Georgetown in a halo of dust, or pitched like a ship in a seaway among the holes and ruts." Quoted in Wake, *Sisters of Fortune*, 59.

299. Pennsylvania Avenue was not paved until 1832. See note 137.

300. Robert Edge Pine (1730–88) was an English artist who painted portraits of Martha Washington's four grandchildren as well as her niece Fanny Bassett during a 1785 visit to Mount Vernon. See Stewart, *Robert Edge Pine*, 50–54. Pine's portraits of Martha and her sister Eleanor "Nelly" Custis Lewis are in Mount Vernon's collection, and the portraits of Elizabeth "Eliza" Custis and George Washington Parke Custis are in the Washington-Custis-Lee Portrait Collection at Washington & Lee University.

301. Martha Washington was actually Britannia's great-grandmother; she died May 22, 1802. George Washington Parke Custis, Britannia's uncle, received "all the family pictures of every sort" per the terms of Martha Washington's will.

302. The Pine portrait of Eleanor "Nelly" Custis Lewis (1779–1852) remained in the Lewis family until it was returned to Mount Vernon in 1922 as a bequest of a descendant.

303. A portrait of Martha Washington's daughter Martha "Patsy" Parke Custis (1756–73), possibly the 1772 portrait miniature by Charles Willson Peale, is now in Mount Vernon's collection that was at Tudor Place and owned by Britannia until 1911. Patsy was actually the younger sister of John Parke Custis (1754–81), Britannia's maternal grandfather. Both were Martha Washington's surviving children from her first marriage to Daniel Parke Custis.

Britannia that she would bequeath to her a collection of letter books containing the correspondence of Eliza Law, written during the time following her separation from her husband, Thomas Law.

At the time of Fanny Lear's death in 1856, Britannia received the two pictures through the efforts of her friend, the former nun Ann Gertrude Wightt. At the time Britannia recounted this information to her grandsons in 1899, the engravings were hanging in the dining room at Tudor Place. They were still hanging there at the time of the 1911 inventory taken of Britannia's estate, which identified them as "Engraving: Captive Frigate *Macedonia*" and "Engraving: *Constitution* and *Guerriere*." Britannia Kennon did not receive the promised books of letters, which instead went to Fanny Lear's niece Louisa Eyre.

Aunt Lewis said she used to say when a girl, that there were things she would never do.[354] One was marry a widower, another was marry a relation of General Washington and the third I cannot remember. All three of which she actually did. Lawrence Lewis was a widower at the time of his marriage to Nellie Custis.[355] Who his first wife was I do not know.[356]

Aunt Lewis used to come down with her two grandsons, the Conrad boys whose mother Angela had died, from Audley every summer and spend several weeks at both Arlington and at Tudor [Place] also at Mrs. Thomson Mason's near Alexandria.[357]

Uncle Lewis died at Arlington while there on a visit & is buried at Mt. Vernon.[358] Aunt Lewis's room at Tudor was the one Agnes now has.[359]

354. Eleanor "Nelly" Custis Lewis (1779–1852), Britannia's aunt.

355. Lawrence Lewis (1767–1839), George Washington's nephew, married Eleanor "Nelly" Custis Lewis at Mount Vernon on February 22, 1799.

356. At the time of his 1799 marriage, Lawrence Lewis was a widower. His first wife, Susannah Edmundson Lewis (ca. 1773–90), died during childbirth.

357. "The Conrad boys" were Lawrence Lewis Conrad (1830–83) and Charles Angelo Conrad (1837–92), both of whom were the sons of Nelly's daughter Mary Eliza Angela Lewis Conrad, who died in 1839. Nelly Lewis was widowed in 1839 and moved permanently to Audley, an estate near Berryville, Virginia, that her husband purchased for their son Lorenzo Lewis. Aside from frequent trips to Louisiana to visit her daughter and grandchildren, Nelly remained at Audley until her death in 1852. See Schmit, *Nelly Custis Lewis's Housekeeping Book*, 16. Elizabeth "Betsey" Clapham Price Mason (1802–73) was the wife of Thompson Mason (1785–1838). The Masons resided at Colross located on Oronoco Street in Alexandria, Virginia. They also owned Huntley, a summer villa located on land that was part of his grandfather George Mason's estate, Gunston Hall.

358. Lawrence Lewis (1767–1839) died at Arlington on November 20, 1839, while there visiting his brother-in-law George Washington Parke Custis. He was buried in the new tomb at Mount Vernon.

359. This statement suggests that Nelly Custis Lewis stayed in the southwest bedroom of Tudor Place when she visited. Armistead Peter 3rd notes this in his book, *Tudor Place*, stating in a passage about the southwest bedroom, "Aunt Lewis, the former Nellie Custis, stayed in this room." Peter, *Tudor Place*, 53.

When Aunt Agnes died I remember going to her funeral [at the] Presbyterian B[urying] G[round].[360] I was walking up and down path in front of the blackbud. [when I] lost [my] gold ring. [The] French attache calling on Meck heard me crying, inquired whether I was hurt.[361] Looked at my finger [and later] brought me ring set with garnet & pearls. Wore it for years the remains are upstairs now.

360. Agnes B. Freeland Peter (1797–1824), the second wife of Britannia's uncle Maj. George Peter, died on May 13, 1824, in her twenty-sixth year (Major Peter's first wife, Ann Plater, died on March 20, 1814, and he married Agnes Buchanan Freeland on July 27, 1815). Britannia would have been eight years old at the time of Agnes's death. The *National Intelligencer* noted, "Died May 13th in Georgetown in the 26th year of her life, Mrs. Agnes Peter, wife of Major George Peter; of a protracted illness. She was a devoted daughter, parent, and wife." Dixon, *National Intelligencer Abstracts, 1824–1826*, 54. The Presbyterian Burying Ground, first established in Georgetown in 1802 on a lot bounded by 4th, 5th, Market, and Frederick Streets (now Volta Place NW, P Street, 33rd, and 34th Streets NW). Burials began at the cemetery in 1806 and continued until 1887. In 1891 between five hundred and seven hundred burials were disinterred and relocated after an attempt was made to demolish the cemetery and use the land for other purposes. At that time Britannia Kennon and several relatives paid to have the remains of their grandparents Robert and Elizabeth Scott Peter and other family members, including Agnes Freeland Peter, moved from the Presbyterian Burying Ground to a new family plot in Georgetown's Oak Hill Cemetery.

361. The "French attaché" is probably Baron Frederick-Franz von Maltitz (1797–1857), a member of the Russian diplomatic delegation whom Britannia incorrectly identified as being French. Maltitz resided in Georgetown and served as acting Russian ambassador to the United States from 1826, following Baron Von Tuyll's recall, until the appointment of Pavel Alexeevich Kridener in 1827. One of Baron Maltitz's calling cards from 1823 survives in the Peter family papers, and he was known to have called on America Pinckney Peter Williams (1803–42), Britannia's older sister.

Mrs. Alexander Hamilton wanted to go to Mt Vernon and asked Mother to go with her.[362] Mr. Cruger, a friend of Mrs. H. went with them, also cousin Abe.[363] Mother's last visit

362. Elizabeth Schuyler Hamilton (1757–1854), widow of Alexander Hamilton, rented Britannia's H Street house. See note 52.

363. The men named here are Bertram Peter Cruger (1774–1854), husband of Mrs. Hamilton's niece Catherine "Kitty" Church Cruger, and Abel Brown Upshur (1821–95), a naval officer who later married Britannia's niece Columbia "Lum" Williams.

made her very sad to go there; everything so changed from when she was a child, When we went to Woodlawn to stay with Aunt & Uncle Lewis we used to drive one day to Mt. Vernon.[364]

December 6, 1900

I often wished that I could go down to "Mount Airy."[365] Mother used to speak of it with such pleasure and of her grandmother & grandfather (Calvert) and the happy days she spent there when a child.[366]

December 7, 1900

Editorial Note: The engraving being discussed in the following paragraph was one that hung in the Tudor Place drawing room during Britannia Kennon's ownership of the house. The engraving by J. C. Buttre, published in 1863, was copied from John Wollaston's 1757 portrait of Martha Dandridge Custis. The original Wollaston portrait of Martha was previously owned by Britannia's uncle George Washington Parke Custis and displayed at Arlington

364. Woodlawn was the estate of Britannia's aunt and uncle Lewis, see note 35. Eleanor "Nelly" Custis Lewis and her husband, Lawrence Lewis, were Britannia's aunt and uncle.

365. Located in Prince George's County, Maryland, Mount Airy was the home of the Calvert family. Originally part of a nine-thousand-acre tract of land that Benedict Swingate Calvert (1722–88) received from his father, Charles Calvert, Fifth Lord Baltimore (1699–1751), in 1751. Mount Airy was Eleanor Calvert Custis Stuart's childhood home.

366. Martha Custis Peter's maternal grandparents were Elizabeth Calvert Calvert (1731–88) and Benedict Swingate Calvert (1722–88). Calvert was the natural son of Charles Calvert, 5th Baron Baltimore, and a descendant of King Charles II.

House. This portrait is now part of the Washington-Custis-Lee Portrait Collection at Washington & Lee University. As Armistead Jr. noted below, William F. Havemeyer, a collector of Washington images, incorrectly postulated that the engraving was President Washington's sister, Elizabeth "Betty" Washington Lewis, rather than Martha Washington.

Armistead Peter Jr. Note: Grandma Says: "It's very strange if that isn't Grandmama Washington's portrait that the original should have hung at Arlington for as many years (for it belonged to Uncle Custis) & that he would not know whose portrait it was."

The above is in regard to the engraving at Mount Vernon and Tudor Place (over the chess men). Mr. Young said Mr. Havemyer (I think) said it was a portrait of Betty Washington.[367] *Compare either miniature with portrait?*[368]

December 9, 1900

Chest of drawers in hall at Tudor Place used to stand in Mr. and Mrs. Washington's room at Mount Vernon.[369] Andirons in the parlor at Tudor in Gen. W's room where he

367. Elizabeth "Betty" Washington Lewis (1733–97), George Washington's sister who resided at Kenmore in Fredericksburg, Virginia, was also the mother of Lawrence Lewis discussed in note 355.

368. This note is a suggestion to compare the engraving in question to two other portrait miniatures of Martha Washington that Britannia also owned. These miniatures, inherited from her mother, Martha Custis Peter, included a 1772 portrait by Charles Willson Peale, and another was an 1801 portrait of the widowed Martha Washington by Robert Field. At the time of Britannia's death, both miniatures were part of the collection of family heirlooms divided among her five grandchildren, and both are now in Mount Vernon's collection.

369. The chest-on-chest was originally commissioned by Washington's neighbor George William Fairfax of Belvoir from London cabinetmaker William Gomm & Sons. Washington purchased the piece at Belvoir in 1774 after Fairfax returned. It was used in the Washingtons' bedchamber at Mount Vernon until his death. In 1802 Britannia's parents, Thomas and Martha Peter, purchased the chest-on-chest for $30.50 at the sale following Martha Washington's death. It has been in its present location in the upper hall at Tudor Place since the late nineteenth century.

died.[370] Plateau at Tudor is <u>the one used</u> at <u>Mt. Vernon</u>.[371] <u>The figures</u> were used on the plateau by him while President in Philadelphia.[372] This plateau was sold as he did not think it was in keeping at Mount Vernon. Originally there were the three large figurines (now on the mantel at Tudor) and twelve small ones—four of which were broken— used last at [my] wedding.[373] <u>The cushions</u> were worked by Grandma Washington <u>after</u> the General's death.[374] There were twelve of them and she gave four to each of her granddaughters.

Armistead Peter Jr. Note: Grandma has the four given to her mother.[375] Cousin Eleanor Goldsboro has one at Mount Vernon but it is in rags.[376]

370. The pair of andirons in the Tudor Place Parlor were also pieces that Thomas and Martha Peter acquired at the 1802 Mount Vernon sale.

371. Britannia inherited six sections of a mirrored mahogany plateau, four of which remain in the Tudor Place collection. This was possibly the plateau appearing on the 1799 inventory at Mount Vernon as "2 Sets Platteaux [s]100" found in the Lumber Room. See "An Inventory of Articles at Mount Vernon" (1799), photocopy in Research Files, Curator's Office, Tudor Place.

372. The Peter family owned several of the biscuit porcelain figurines acquired in 1790 by Gouverneur Morris in Paris for President and Mrs. Washington. Britannia displayed one of the figures, "Venus and Two Cupids," on the mantel in the Tudor Place drawing room. After Britannia's death in 1911 the figurines were part of the family collection that was divided among her five grandchildren, and the figurines are now in Mount Vernon's collection. See Cadou, *George Washington Collection*, 142.

373. Britannia W. Peter married Beverley Kennon at Tudor Place on December 8, 1842.

374. In 1765 Martha Washington ordered materials in order to make "one dozen chair bottoms"—cushions for twelve Windsor chairs used at Mount Vernon. She worked on the cushions for the next thirty-six years, cross-stitching a repeating motif of scallop shells in red multistrand worsted wool and yellow silk thread on a casing of yellow worsted wool to which hand-knotted silk and wool fringe was added. See Cadou, *George Washington Collection*, 200.

One of the four embroidered cushions made by Martha Washington that Britannia inherited from her mother and described to her grandchildren. Collection of Tudor Place Historic House & Garden. Photograph by Bruce White.

January 28, 1901

Aunt Custis (Mrs. Law) lived at Peter Grove.[404] After that on 1st Street where the Laird's lived.[405] Mother left Sister America and I there with her for a few days when she went to Oakland.[406] After that Aunt Custis lived in the Six Buildings then she went up to some of the V[irgini]a Springs, then she went to Richmond to visit her friends Mr. and Mrs. Chevalier, where she died.[407] He accompanied her remains to Alexandria and from there they went to Mt. Vernon where they were placed in the vault.

404. Peter Grove, the estate of Britannia's uncle David Peter. See note 27.

405. Present-day N Street NW in Georgetown. See appendix 1.

406. On Oakland, see note 185.

407. The Six Buildings was a group of row houses located on the north side of Pennsylvania Avenue between 21st and 22nd Streets NW that were constructed ca. 1800 by Washington real estate speculator James Greenleaf. See Goode, *Capital Losses*, 140. In the western part of the state of Virginia (including what is now West Virginia) were several resort hotels associated with mineral springs. These resorts were popular destinations for travelers who sought to improve their health by drinking and bathing in the waters. The resorts were also social destinations for the southern aristocracy prior to the Civil War. See Lewis, *Ladies and Gentlemen on Display* for a discussion of the social aspects of these visits. On Jean Auguste Marie Chevillié and his wife, Catherine Power Chevallié of Richmond, see note 345.

February 16, 1901

[The] surgeon [of the] U.S. Army in charge of one of the hospitals in the city, Dr. and Mrs. Hornor were staying here during the war with their little son Mackie Hornor.[408] The feeling was very strong at that time between the North & South. Of course they were Northern people Mackie knowing that I was a southerner asked his mother . . . "don't you think if Mrs.

408. This suggests that Dr. Caleb W. Hornor (1825–1903) and his wife, Julia Marie Washington Hornor (1828–1914) were among the tenants renting rooms from Britannia Kennon at Tudor Place at some point between the summer of 1862 and the end of the war in the spring of 1865. Following the end of the Civil War, Dr. Hornor was appointed chief medical officer of the Freedman's Bureau, the government agency within the War Department that was established to assist millions of formerly enslaved African Americans in the South. Their son was William MacPherson "Mackie" Hornor (1860–1937). See note 326.

Kennon was to die that she would go to heaven?" His mother told him yes.

Years after he and his mother came to W[ashington] and came over to see me and when I told him about what he had said he seemed much mortified at having said such a thing & hoped I would not think of it again. I told him I have always treasured it & shall never forget it for it was a sweet thought from a child.

February 17, 1901

Letters of Washington to Eliza Custis concerning her prospective marriage was given to Mother by Lewis Washington when he sold W[ashington]'s papers to the Govt.[409] this & one other to Aunt Lewis were found & he sent them to mother.[410] She gave Aunt Lewises to her & she burned it with the other letters from Washington.[411]

409. Elizabeth "Eliza" Custis Law (1776–1831) was Britannia's aunt. This is a reference to a series of letters written by President Washington to his step-granddaughter with advice about relationships and marriage. "Mother" is Martha Custis Peter (1777–1854), Britannia's mother. Lewis William Washington (1812–71) was a grandnephew of George Washington. Through his father and other relatives, he inherited papers and objects formerly owned by his great-uncle George Washington. It was actually George Corbin Washington, Lewis William Washington's father, who sold President Washington's papers to the US government in 1834. These papers are now found in the Library of Congress. However, in 1871 Lewis William Washington's widow sold his collection of President Washington's papers and artifacts to the State of New York. These objects now reside in the collection of the New York State Library. See Toner, "Some Account of George Washington's Library," 96–98.

410. The September 14, 1794, letter from George Washington to Eliza Custis, in which he gives her advice on marriage, remained in the Peter family's collection at Tudor Place until Britannia's death in 1911. It's now part of the collection of the Fred W. Smith National Library for the Study of George Washington at Mount Vernon. "Aunt Lewis" is Eleanor "Nelly" Custis Lewis, and "Mother" is Martha Custis Peter.

411. While Britannia states that her aunt Eleanor "Nelly" Custis Lewis burned many of these letters, at least one letter exists in fragmentary state that is now in

the collection of the Bodlean Library, Oxford University—Washington's letter to Eleanor "Nelly" Parke Custis, March 21, 1796. The same letter, though incorrectly dated, was included in the 1861 book of reminiscences of Nelly's brother George Washington Parke Custis, *Recollections of Washington* (Philadelphia, 1861) compiled by Mary Anna Randolph Custis Lee. A blog entry by Jennifer Stertzer on The Papers of George Washington website discusses the re-attributed date of this letter and its contents. See Stertzer, "George Washington to Eleanor 'Nelly' Parke Custis, 21 March 1796."

April 11, 1901

When Gen[eral] Fitzhugh Lee was writing the life of his illustrious kinsman h[is] wife wrote to [me] at his request to inquire <u>who</u> the clergyman was who performed the marriage ceremony.[412] [I] said at once that it was Rev. Ruel Keith but before replying had verified the fact by looking up the marriage notice in the *National Intelligencer*.[413] Several clergymen have been given the honor of having performed the ceremony—among them the Rev. Mr. Meade afterwards Bishop of Virginia.[414]

They were married in the parlor at Arlington (on the right as you enter the front door). The room back of the parlor was never finished until Cousin Robert had it plastered, although it was occasionally used as a dining room by Uncle Custis.[415]

412. Fitzhugh Lee (1835–1905) was a nephew of Robert E. Lee who also served a Confederate general during the Civil War. He was later the governor of Virginia and a general in the US Army during the Spanish-American War. In 1869 he published *General Lee*, a biography of his uncle. Fitzhugh Lee's wife was Ellen Bernard Fowle Lee (1853–1933).

413. Rev. Reuel Keith (1792–1842), see note 400.

414. Rev. William Mead (1789–1862) served as assistant bishop of the Episcopal Diocese of Virginia from 1829 to 1841 and as bishop of the Episcopal Diocese of Virginia from 1841 until 1862. Mead was a cousin of Mrs. Custis, the bride's mother, so this may be why he was incorrectly credited with marrying the Lees.

415. Britannia's cousin Mary Anna Custis Lee became the owner of Arlington House upon the death of her father, George Washington Parke Custis, in 1857. Her husband, Robert E. Lee, took a two-year leave of absence from the US Army to settle the estate of his late father-in-law and manage the large plantation.

December 4, 1901

Cousin Lorenzo Lewis, Cousin Robert Lee (both of whom were staying here & both married) and brother—the one and only time I ever went to the theater without a chaperone.[416] Will Johnson driving & Jisey footman [Illeg] from the box the horses pulled the pole out.[417] Ran into lamps lighted in front of President's house.[418]

416. Lorenzo Lewis (1803–47) was Britannia's first cousin; see note 402. Robert E. Lee (1807–70) was the husband of Britannia's cousin Mary Anna Custis Lee. "Brother" here is probably Britannia's brother George Washington Peter (1801–77).

417. Will Johnson was the Peter family's enslaved coachman; see note 5. The enslaved footman rode at the rear of the coach.

418. Britannia suggests that the horses were tied to a light post on Lafayette Square, something startled them, causing them to flee, and the pole was subsequently pulled out of the ground.

February 23, 1902

George Bancroft, Secy. of the Navy came to Tudor to see me about Bev's appointment in the Navy.[419] We walked down to the little arbor[420] & Mr. B. told me that while he had no appointments at his disposal at the time, if I would send Bev. to Indiana and have him reside there 6 mos. he would give him a fractional appointment—which he did in less than 6 mo[nths] I believe. I told Mr. B. that I thought while I was most anxious for & wanted the appointment, I thought it was a gross infringement of the law.

419. George Bancroft (1800–1891) served as secretary of the navy from March 11, 1845, to September 9, 1846. His most notable accomplishment during his tenure as secretary of the navy was the establishment of the US Naval Academy at Annapolis, Maryland. The subject of this passage is Bancroft's visit to Tudor Place regarding an appointment for Britannia's stepson Beverley "Bev" Kennon Jr. (1830–90) to the academy. Bancroft would have known Britannia's late husband, Beverley Kennon, as both were high-ranking officials in the Navy Department. The eldest son of Cdre. Beverley Kennon and his first wife, Elizabeth Dandridge Claiborne Kennon, "Bev," as he was called by the family, served in the US Navy from 1846 to 1861 before resigning his commission to join the Confederate Navy. He later served as a mercenary for the Khedive of Egypt.

420. A landscape feature in the Tudor Place garden.

bushes of roses to make one bottle of rose water, about a q[uar]t after it was made she would keep one bottle and send mother the other. Coconut Cakes—[cost] quarter of a dollar a dozen, some pink and some white.

*Such a thing as a gentlemen presenting candy to a young lady in those days was unheard of—A single japonica was considered a marked attention and as there was but one florist here—Pierce's Gardeners—in the upper part of what is now the city of Washington a gentleman had quite a ride even to secure that— $1.00 each usually.[475]

475. Joshua Pierce (1795–1869) operated the first general nursery in the District of Columbia and provided botanical specimens for the grounds of the US Capitol building, the President's House, and many of the city's other parks. His estate, Linnaean Hill, in Northwest Washington included his residence, greenhouses, and gardens. He had additional nurseries on a fifty-four-acre parcel of land in Northwest Washington between R and S Streets. See Bushong, *Historic Resources Study: Rock Creek Park*, 30.

September 16, 1908

I have that confidence in my ancestors & I believe in their strict [illeg] & that they valued what they were doing. I am a Federalist of '76. I didn't say that I was a believer in Alex[ander] Hamilton but I certainly am not of T[homas] J[efferson].

Undated

Baron Maltitze,* a Russian, and a member of the legation, was devoted to "Meck."[476] On one occasion, as they were walking through the garden, he asked her to give him as many gooseberries as there were days that she wished him to be absent![477] "Meck" picked a handful and gave them to him, and he put them into his pocket. Two days later he was back at "Tudor" again. Some reference was made to the gooseberries, and he said: "Oh! But I did have them made into one pie!"

*Armistead Peter Jr. Note. *Grandmother is not sure that his name is correctly spelled.*

476. Baron Frederick-Franz von Maltitz (1797–1857), see note 361.

477. Gooseberry is a fruit, *Ribes uva-crispa*, related to the currant.

Undated

Early in the Civil War it was found that the soldiers were pillaging Arlington and Markie got an order from Genl. Scott and had the things there packed and brought here—two great wagon loads—and here they remained in the garret until the war was over.[478]

478. Arlington House, the estate of Mr. and Mrs. Robert E. Lee. "Markie" here is Martha Custis Williams Carter (1827–99), Britannia's niece, who lived at Tudor Place from 1838 to 1852 and later resided at Arlington House and acted as a companion for her great-uncle George Washington Parke Custis from 1853 to 1857, so she would have been familiar with the house and the Custis-Lee family's collection of Washington heirlooms. General Winfield Scott, see note 81. As Britannia notes, portions of the Custis-Lee family collection were stored in the Tudor Place attic for much of the Civil War.

Martha Carter—

    Terry Sinclair—bro. of Dr.

Sinclair[480]

    Gilberta Sinclair—niece of

Grandpa[481]

    William Kennon—son of

Erasmus[482]

    Mr. Cazenove

    Harriet Stuart

    Lewis Warrington[483]

    Niece of Grandpa—Rebecca

Kennon

    Wm Chandler[484]

    Henrietta Dunlop[485]

    Elizabeth Johnson[486]

    Mary Chandler

    Abel B. Upshur[487]

    Thursday, December 8th at 7:30

p.m.[488]

479. The wedding party for the December 8, 1841, marriage of Britannia W. Peter to Cdre. Beverley Kennon, which took place in the Tudor Place drawing room at 7:30 p.m.

480. Martha "Markie" Custis Williams Carter (1827–99); George Terry Sinclair (1816–85), nephew of Cdre. Beverley Kennon (see note 70) and Dr. William B. Sinclair (1818–95) of Norfolk, Virginia, Commodore Kennon's nephew. Sinclair served as a surgeon in both the US Navy and later the Confederate Navy.

481. Gilberta Sinclair Whittle (1824–1906) was the daughter of Arthur and Sarah Skipwith Sinclair and a niece of Cdre. Beverley Kennon. Gilberta married Dr. Conway Davies Whittle Jr.

482. William Henry Kennon (1832–76), nephew of Commodore Beverley Kennon, was the son of Erasmus Kennon (1786-1840), brother of Commodore Beverley Kennon. See note 442.

483. Louis Sebert "Albert" Cazenove (1807–52) would later marry Harriet Eugenia Calvert Stuart (1823–96) in 1850. Harriet was the daughter of Charles Calvert, Martha Custis Peter's half-brother. Lewis Warrington (1782–1852) was a US Navy officer who served as commandant of the Norfolk Navy Yard and later chief of the Bureau of Yards and Docks. For a month following the February 1844 death of Navy Secretary Thomas Walker Gilmer, Warrington served as the acting secretary of the navy.

484. Rebecca Kennon Mayo (1825–78), Beverley Kennon's niece, was a daughter of Dr. George T. Kennon. She married Abel U. Mayo of Richmond, Virginia, in 1861. William Chandler (1812–92) was a US naval officer who served with Beverley Kennon.

485. Henrietta Johnson Dunlop (1813–93), Britannia's first cousin, was the daughter of James and Elizabeth Peter Dunlop.

486. It's unclear as to whether this is Elizabeth Dunlop Johnson (1790–1846), Britannia's first cousin and daughter of James and Elizabeth Peter Dunlop, or her daughter of the same name, Elizabeth Johnson Lowry (1815–88), who, though being Britannia Kennon's first cousin once removed, was the same age as Britannia.

487. Mary Chandler of Georgetown was the sister of Capt. William Chandler, mentioned in note 484. Abel B. Upshur (1821–95) was a naval officer and the cousin of Secretary of State Abel P. Upshur, who died aboard the *Princeton* with Commodore Kennon in 1844. In 1872 Abel B. Upshur married Britannia's niece Columbia Williams in Baltimore. See Historical Records Survey of Virginia Service Division and the Works Projects Administration, *Index to Marriage Notices in the Southern Churchman, 1835–1941*, 240.

488. The date and time of Britannia and Beverley Kennon's wedding.

The first school I went to was kept by Miss Mary & Miss Isabella Wright, two old maids.[489] The school was on 1st St. in Smith row end house.[490] Gen. McComb was next door & next to him lived Col. Roberdeau, next to him afterwards the Van Deventers—who later lived in the Linthicum place.[491] Madam Iturbide lived in that row—where cousin W[illia]m Laird lived.[492] Miss Wright kept school in corner house this end. The Schaaffs lived where Mr. Barber lives now.[493] Mrs. S[chaff] was Mr. Schaaff's second wife.[494] He had 3 dau[ghter]s & 2 sons.

489. Mary and Isabella Wright operated a school on 1st Street (now N Street) in Georgetown west of Wisconsin Avenue; see appendix 1. Receipts for Britannia's tuition at the school in the Peter family papers suggest that she attended the school from 1823 to 1825.

490. A row of townhouses on 1st Street was constructed in 1810 by Clement and Walter Smith. As Britannia discusses, the school run by the Wright sisters was in the end building at the intersection of what is now N Street and Potomac Street NW.

491. Other residents of Smith Row are also described. Gen. Alexander Macomb (1782–1841) was the commanding general of the US Army from 1828 to 1841. Col. Isaac Roberdeau (1763–1829), surveyor, cartographer, and head of the Army's Topographical Bureau, resided in Georgetown with his wife, Susan Shippen Blair Roberdeau. Maj. Christopher Van Deventer (1788–1838) was the chief clerk of the War Department.

492. Linthicum Place was the estate located across Road Street from Tudor Place. It was purchased in 1846 by Edward Magruder Linthicum. In the late 1820s Major Van Deventer leased the Road Street estate from its previous owner, John C. Calhoun, before purchasing a house on First (now N) Street. Ana María de Huarte y Muñiz Iturbide (1786–1861) was the consort of Emperor Augustin I of Mexico; see note 213. William Laird (1800–1874; see note 422) married Britannia's cousin Helen Dunlop in 1822, and this is why she identifies him as "cousin William Laird."

493. Dr. John Thomas Schaaff (1752/53–1819), his second wife, Mary Stewart Schaaff (1773–1860), and their children from his previous marriage resided at No. 26 1st Street (now N Street) between High (Wisconsin Ave) and Market Streets (33rd Street) in Georgetown. Dr. Schaaff was a graduate of the University of Edinburgh and was described in his 1819 *National Intelligencer* obituary as "a physician of celebrity and a gentleman of high standing in society." See Castle, "Life in Georgetown, 1819–1841." "Mr. Barber" is probably John Adlum Barber (1838–1905), the only surviving child of Col. Cornelius Barber (1803–53) and his wife, Margaret Adlum Barber (1810–92). John Barber was the only one of the five Barber children to survive the 1849 cholera epidemic, during which all four of his sisters died during the same week.

494. As Britannia notes, Mary Stewart Schaaff was Dr. Schaaff's second wife. Dr. Schaaff first married Mary Sydebothan (1776–1810) in 1800, and, two years after her death in 1810, he married Mary Stewart in Ann Arundel County, Maryland. The five children mentioned by Britannia in this passage were from Dr. Schaaff's first marriage.

Jane—Mr. Bishop Johns[495]

Ann (Miss)[496]

Mary m. Mr. Stevenson who had been in Congress & Minister to England.[497]

Arthur m. Miss Mary Forsyth dau. of Sen. Forsyth of Georgia (who was afterwards Sec. of State under Van Buren).[498] He lived in Col[umbian] Hospital.[499]

Charles—never married.[500]

495. In 1838 Margaretta Jane Schaaff (d. 1854) married Bishop John Johns (1796–1876), the fourth Episcopal bishop of Virginia and later the fifteenth president of the College of William and Mary from 1849 to 1854. Johns was a widower when he married Jane, as his previous wife had died in 1836. Following Jane's death in 1854, Johns married Angelina Southgate.

496. Ann Schaaff (1805–62) never married. Her surviving correspondence is the subject of Guy Castle's "Life in Georgetown, 1819–1841, as Told in the Personal Correspondence of Ann Schaaff."

497. Mary Schaaff (1820–65) married former diplomat Andrew Stevenson in 1849. Stevenson was a widower whose second wife died the previous year. Following Andrew Stevenson's death in 1857, Mary returned to Georgetown and lived with her sister until her 1865 death. Andrew Stevenson (1784–1857) was the US minister to the United Kingdom from 1836 to 1841 and a former US representative from Virginia. Mary Schaaff was Stevenson's third wife. He was previously married to Mary Page White from 1809 to 1812 and Sarah Coles from 1816 to 1848. See Wayland, *Andrew Stevenson*, 12, 40, 214.

498. Arthur Schaaff (1804–34) worked as a clerk at the US Department of State when his father-in-law, John Forsyth (1780–1841) of Georgia, served as secretary of state. Prior to his appointment as secretary of state by President Andrew Jackson, Forsyth served in the US House of Representatives 1813–18 and 1823–27, and as US senator 1818–19 and again 1829–34. See Dodge et al., eds., *Biographical Directory of the United States Congress, 1774–2005*, 1073. John's daughter Mary Athenia Forsyth (1807–78) married Arthur Schaaff in 1824. Martin Van Buren was the eighth president of the United States, in office from March 4, 1837, to March 4, 1841.

499. Britannia suggests that Arthur Schaaff lived for a time at Columbian Hospital but doesn't state why. Columbian Hospital was located on the campus of Columbian College. Following the outbreak of the Civil War, many of the students left Columbian College and joined the Confederate Army. Buildings on the campus were then used as military hospitals. The college's campus was located in the Columbian Heights neighborhood of Washington, DC. In 1873 Columbian College relocated to a campus at 15th and H Streets NW, and in 1909 the college was renamed George Washington University.

500. Charles Schaaff (1810–40).

Undated

The white plates with broad gilt band at Tudor were purchased by Aunt Law for a dinner she gave at Peter's Grove to Lafayette in [18]24.[501] The table was in the shape of a horse-shoe. When she left Georgetown she wanted to dispose of the plates & Mother bought them.[502]

501. "Aunt Law" is Elizabeth "Eliza" Custis Law (1776–1831), Britannia's aunt. The plates mentioned by Britannia, which Martha Peter purchased from her sister Eliza, are still in the Tudor Place collection. At the time of Lafayette's 1824 visit to Georgetown, Eliza Custis Law was renting Peter Grove, a house in Georgetown on Road Street that was originally constructed by Britannia's uncle David Peter.

502. Britannia's mother, Martha Custis Peter.

Undated

Took Mother and Father 4 days to drive to Phila[delphia].[503] Mr. and Mrs. James Gibson also Mrs. Joshua Fisher.[504] They invited me to spend the evening—they were old people and contemporaries of mother and Aunt Lewis[505]—Mother made their acquaintance while staying with Gen. & Mrs. Washington.

503. Britannia's mother, Martha Custis Peter, and father, Thomas Peter.

504. James Gibson (1769–1856) and his wife, Elizabeth Bordley Gibson (1777–1863; see note 332); and Elizabeth Powell Francis Fisher (1777–1855; see note 335).

505. Eleanor "Nelly" Custis Lewis (1779–1852), Britannia's aunt.

Undated

Editorial Note: In the undated paragraph below, Britannia describes the enslaved individuals she recalled at Tudor Place during her childhood.

11 Servants [at Tudor Place]. [I was] accustomed to servants from my earliest childhood. 5 horses—2 carriage horses, brothers each had a riding horse & also father ([his horse was named] "Dobbin"[506]) Will Twine worked garden & nothing else.[507] Man & a boy latter went with carriage as footman. Will Johnson was coachman. Poor old Patty cook[508]— wood fire here at [first] light in the morning. Elvy[509]—waited on Sister America. Nancey the laundress.[510] Annie[511]—seamstress lived in house in corner of lot. She had a dau[ghter]. Dau[ghter] & a boy—Little Jack Gray.

Beauty and the Beast: Count Bodisco of Russia, a very polished man entertained handsomely waltzed beautifully.[512] He married Harriet Williams, married at old Williams house on Road St.[513] After the marriage he took his bride directly home on 2nd

506. Here Britannia states that her father Thomas Peter rode a horse named "Dobbins."

507. Will Twine (1784–1832) was the Peter family's enslaved gardener.

508. Patty Allen, the Peter family's enslaved cook; see note 3.

509. Elvy (ca. 1789–?), was a lady's maid for Britannia's sister America P. Peter. Elvy appears on the 1796 patrimony list of Custis dower slaves, which notes her age then as seven years old and value as £23. Presuming she was transferred to America P. Peter at the time of her 1826 marriage to William G. Williams, Elvy would have been thirty-seven years old at that time.

510. Nothing is known about Nancey except her role as the Peter family's enslaved laundress at Tudor Place.

511. Annie Gray (dates unknown) was the Peter family's enslaved seamstress at Tudor Place. She lived in a small wooden building located on the northeast corner of the Tudor Place property with two children.

512. Count Aleksandr Andreevitch de Bodisco (1786–1854) was the envoy extraordinary and minister plenipotentiary to the United States from Russia, serving in that capacity from 1837 until his death in 1854. He is best remembered for his 1840 marriage to a sixteen-year-old Georgetown schoolgirl, Harriet Williams, whom Britannia describes in this passage.

513. Harriet Beall Williams de Bodisco Scott (1824–90) was a sixteen-year-old schoolgirl when she married Bodisco, the fifty-four-year-old Russian ambassador, on April 16, 1840 (see note 512). Seven years after his 1854 death, Harriet married Capt. Douglas Scott, a British army officer she met during a tour of India, at the residence of her parents, located on Road (now R) Street in Georgetown.

street next to Ottley's house.[514] They had quite a large family all of whom are dead.[515] Count Bodisco had living with him two nephews, Vladimir and Boris.[516] Vladimir m[arried] a Russian lady & had three sons.[517] He resided in different places, a time in the Cissel house [on] 31st street.[518] His widow left for Russia to visit her mother taking with her two sons, all were lost in English Channel.[519] The one child that she left here is Caroline who married Brooke Williams, is in the Louise Home.[520]

While I was at school at the convent Mrs. Lee (R. E. Lee's mother) lived there[521]—after that Mr. Forsythe Senator from Georgia lived there for some years.[522] These prior to Bodiscos.

514. The Bodisco House is located on O Street between 34th and 35th Streets in Georgetown. Following the April 16, 1840, ceremony, a wedding breakfast was held at the Bodisco residence. For a description of the house and the history of its ownership, see Lebovich, "Bodisco House (Clement Smith House)." As noted in appendix 1, the name of 2nd street was changed to O Street in 1895.

515. Aleksandr de Bodisco was a widower with one son when he married Harriet Williams in 1840. Count de Bodisco and Harriet Williams de Bodisco had six additional children prior to his death in 1854.

516. Waldemar de Bodisco (1825–78), a nephew of Baron de Bodisco who accompanied his uncle to Georgetown, graduated from Georgetown College in 1848, and then served as secretary of the Russian Legation in Washington for nearly twenty years. In 1871 he was appointed consul general in New York and served in that position until his death in 1878. See Wilson and Fiske, *Appleton's Cyclopedia of American Biography*, 1:299. Another of Baron de Bodisco's nephews was Boris de Bodisco (1801–28).

517. Annette de Bodisco, the 1860 US Census notes, was born in Poland, then a part of the Russian Empire. A distant cousin of her husband, Waldemar de Bodisco, she came to Georgetown following their marriage. Lillard, *Here Come the Russians*. The three sons of Waldemar de Bodisco were Alexander de Bodisco (1858–78), Waldemar/Voldemar Peter Bodisco (1850–?), and Boris Karl Bodisco (1851–78).

518. The "Cissel House," now known as the Williams-Addison House, is located directly across 31st street from Tudor Place. The 1863 Washington City Directory lists Bodisco as residing here, described as on Congress Street (now 31st) between P and R Streets.

519. His widow is Anna Catharine Von Dolst Bodisco (1826–78). As Britannia describes in this passage, Mrs. Bodisco and two of her three sons (Alexander Bodisco and Boris de Bodisco; see note 517) died on November 25, 1878, in the sinking of the *Pomerania*, a Hamburg-Amerika Line steamship that was struck on the starboard side by another vessel while crossing the English Channel. The *Pomerania* sank less than half an hour later. See "The Sunken Steamer," *Times* [Philadelphia], November 28, 1878, p. 1.

520. Caroline Bodisco Williams (1829–1900) was the daughter of Waldemar de Bodisco and the wife of Brooke Beall Williams Jr. (1828–94), the son of Brooke Williams (1790–1843) and Rebecca Beck Williams (1804–80). The Louise Home was a home for aged and destitute women; see note 133. Caroline Bodisco Williams likely resided in the Louise Home for the last few years of her life after the death of her husband.

521. In 1825 Anne Hill Carter Lee (1773–1829), the widowed mother of Robert E. Lee, moved from Alexandria to Georgetown, where her son Charles Carter Lee practiced law.

522. John Forsyth (1781–1841), see note 498.

Linthicum House:[523] I have heard mother say that she did not know who built the house.[524] The first occupants that mother knew anything about were Mr. and Mrs. Robert Beverley.[525] Mother knew Mrs. Beverley very well and was very intimate with her.[526] Blandfield Virginia was his house.[527]

William—bachelor lived & died at Blandfield[528]

Bradshaw—married Jane Peter[529]

Maria—married Dr. Clark[530]

Roberta—married Mr. Lightfoot[531]

Mrs. Beverley died & Mr. Beverley came to town & lived with his daughter Mrs. Clark.[532]

I can enumerate a great many who lived there but the succession may not be correct.

523. The estate now known as Dumbarton Oaks was located across Road Street from Tudor Place. During Britannia's childhood the estate occupied an entire block until the 1854 sale of the northernmost portion of the lot.

524. "Mother" here is Martha Custis Peter (1777–1854), Britannia's mother. James H. Dorsey constructed the earliest portion of the house at Dumbarton Oaks in 1801. Four years later the widower Dorsey sold the house and property to Robert Beverley.

525. Robert Beverley (1769–1843) and his wife, Jane Tayloe Beverley (1774–1816). Robert Beverley purchased the property from James H. Dorsey in 1805 and owned it until 1822 when it was sold to the Calhouns.

526. Jane Tayloe Beverley was the sister of Col. John Tayloe III.

527. Blandfield was the Essex County, Virginia, estate of the Beverley family; see note 262.

528. William Bradshaw Beverley (1791–1866) died at Selma in Loudon County, Virginia, in 1866, not at Blandfield as Britannia stated here. See McGill, *Beverley Family of Virginia*, 551–52.

529. James Bradshaw Beverley (1797–1853) married Britannia's first cousin Jane Johns Peter (1800–1863) on May 6, 1819. She was the daughter of David Peter and Sarah Johns Peter.

530. Maria Beverley Clarke (1791–aft. 1860), daughter of Robert Beverley and Jane Tayloe Beverley (see note 263) married Dr. George Clarke (1789–1822) of Georgetown. He died of typhoid fever during an outbreak at Blandfield in October 1822 after traveling there to treat his sisters-in-law, Rebecca and Jane Beverley, who also died during the outbreak (see note 532). See McGill, *Beverley Family of Virginia*, 551.

531. Roberta Beverley Lightfoot (?–1834), daughter of Robert Beverley and Jane Tayloe Beverley, married William Bernard Lightfoot (1811–70) in 1834 and died suddenly several months later.

532. Robert Beverley (1769–1843) came to Georgetown following the death of his wife, Jane Tayloe Beverley (1774–1816), to reside with his daughter, Maria Beverley Clarke, and her husband. Maria Clarke was widowed in October 1822 after her husband, Dr. Clarke, contracted typhoid fever while treating her two sisters during an outbreak at Blandfield. The incident is noted in an 1822 newspaper article in the *Richmond Enquirer* that was subsequently reprinted across the country: "A mortality has afflicted the family of Blandfield, in the county of Essex [Virginia]. . . . One of the interesting daughters was the first to fall a victim. A second soon followed her to the tomb. Dr. George Clarke, a son in law, and a highly esteemed physician of Georgetown, visited the family to administer his professional services and shared the same fate on last Saturday week." See "Distressing Visitation," *Vermont Gazette*, November 5, 1822, p. 2.

Mrs. Calhoun, the mother of John C. Calhoun lived there in 1824 when Lafayette was in the country.[533] John C. Calhoun & wife lived there with his mother & as Secy of War tendered Lafayette a reception.[534] Father & Mother went & took me. I was a little thing at the time.[535]

Prussian Minister Baron Greuhm lived there.[536] He died there & his remains are interred in Congressional Cemetery in Washington.[537] Mother had been very polite to her (Baroness Greuhm[538]) and when she left she gave mother the Crystal with medallion head of Washington in it (now in the cabinet).[539]

Major & Mrs. Van Deventer & their family lived there:[540]
{Marcia[541]

533. It was actually John C. Calhoun's mother-in-law, Floride Rebecca Bonneau Colhoun (1770–1836), widow of Senator John Ewing Colhoun of South Carolina. John C. Calhoun's mother, Martha Caldwell Calhoun, died in South Carolina in 1802. Floride Bonneau Colhoun purchased the Georgetown property in 1823 and resided there with her son-in-law and his family until 1829 when the property was sold to James Bradshaw Beverley.

534. On John C. Calhoun, see note 103. Floride Bonneau Colhoun (1792–1866), daughter of John Ewing Colhoun and Floride Rebecca Bonneau Colhoun, was the wife of John C. Calhoun, who was also her first cousin once removed.

535. Britannia was nine years old at the time of Lafayette's visit to Georgetown in October 1824.

536. Friedrich von Greuhm (1780–1823) was a Prussian diplomat. Von Greuhm served as the first minister resident and consul-general to the United States from Prussia, 1817–23.

537. Von Greuhm died at his residence in Georgetown on December 1, 1823, and his funeral was held on December 4. Congress recessed so members could attend the service. See "Death of the Russian [sic] Minister," *New England Farmer*, December 13, 1823, p. 159.

538. Virginie Bridon de Greuhm (1794–1860), was born in Paris and married Baron de Greuhm in Washington in 1819. Two years after his 1823 death, she married Luke E. Lawless (1781–1846) in Georgetown, and they later moved to St. Louis, Missouri. Lawless was a British-born lawyer who practiced law in England and France before he immigrated to the United States in 1816, where he practiced law and later received an appointment to the Third Judicial Circuit of the State of Missouri. She was later known as Virginia de Greuhm Lawless. See Bailey, *Charleston Belles Abroad*, 251n43.

539. The framed sulfide profile of President Washington hung in the Tudor Place Parlor until the division of the collection following Britannia's death in 1911.

540. Maj. Christopher Van Deventer (1788–1838) was chief clerk of the War Department during Calhoun's tenure as Secretary of War. He actually married three times: first to Marcia Kellogg (1789–1813), with whom he had a one child; then to Eliza Cooper (1785–1819), with whom he had one child; and finally in 1823 to Sally Birkhead (1796–1874), with whom he had additional children. Van Deventer resided on this property from July 1826 until his dismissal from the War Department in 1827; see Lebovich, "Bodisco House," 7, for a discussion of Van Deventer's time renting the property. Van Deventer was dismissed from the War Department after a scandal in which his brother-in-law was awarded a construction contract and then he assumed a financial interest in the project.

541. Marcia Van Deventer Stevens, the daughter of Maj. Christopher Van Deventer and his first wife, Marcia Kellogg Van Deventer. She married Eugene Stevens. See Van Deventer, *Van Deventer Family*, 43.

Eugene[542]

Liza} sister America & I knew them very well[543]

And an adopted daughter, Miss Antoinette Grennell.[544]

Brooke Mackall lived there and he turned it into a truck garden but didn't live there very long.[545] Fish, awful mammals, & it was awful. Then Linthicum bought it.[546]

542. Eugene Winfield Scott Van Deventer (1815–54) was the son of Maj. Christopher Van Deventer and his second wife, Eliza Cooper Van Deventer. Eugene, like his father, was a career military officer and served as captain of a Michigan regiment in Gen. Franklin Pierce's brigade during the Mexican War.

543. Eliza J. Hyde Van Deventer (1816–1906) and Eugene W. S. Van Deventer married on September 10, 1838, and eventually had three children. See Van Deventer, *Van Deventer Family*, 43.

544. Antoinette Grennell (1809–62) was the adopted daughter of Maj. Christopher Van Deventer. She died in Buffalo, New York in 1862. See Wilson, *Knox County, Tennessee Bible Records*.

545. Brooke Mackall (1801–80) owned the property being discussed from 1826 to 1846 and grew produce that was sold locally in a market garden.

546. Edward Magruder Linthicum purchased the property in 1846, first naming the estate Monterrey after the Mexican war battle in which his son was killed, but he later changed the name to "The Oaks." Linthicum died in 1869, and his widow remained on the property until her death in 1884, at which point the property was inherited by their adopted grandson Edward Linthicum Dent.

Undated, Montrose [547]

Old Mr. Parrot built "Montrose" (& then it was sold, Mr. Clem. Smith[548] bought it).[549] When Mr. Parrot lived there, he had a rope walk.[550] Clem

547. Located on Road (now R) Street, Montrose was an estate that abutted The Oaks and was also across the street from David Peter's Peter Grove. Industrialist Richard Parrot acquired the property through three conveyances between 1804 and 1813, naming it Elderslie. He built a Federal style house on the property in 1810, and it was a later owner, William Boyce, who named the estate Montrose. The house was razed in 1911, and the site is now the location of Montrose Park. See Architrave P.C., et al., *Montrose Park*.

548. Clement Smith (1776–1839), the president of the Farmers and Mechanics Bank of Georgetown, purchased the property in 1822.

549. Richard Parrot (1766–1823), was a Georgetown industrialist who owned a rope-making business and a mill.

550. After purchasing the property in 1804, Richard Parrot constructed a ropewalk on the east side of his property that became known as Parrot's Woods, where hemp was hand twisted to manufacture the ropes needed on the docks and wharves of Georgetown. Typical ropewalks were seven hundred to nine hundred feet in length. As part of the manufacturing process, the rope was dipped in hot tar as a preservative, and the large tar kettles would have given off a strong odor and were fire hazards. Parrot's ropewalk was burned by the British in 1814. See Architrave P.C., et al., *Montrose Park*.

Smith's family lived there for a number of years.[551]

George Croghn bought it & lived there & then Capt. Boyce bought it.[552] Capt. Boyce was in partnership with Mr. Vincent Taylor—Millers.[553] Taylor attended to the milling and Boyce to the financial part.

Captain Boyce married Miss McEwen of Phila[delphia].[554] Very pretty, considered a great beauty & so ladylike.

551. The Clement Smith family owned the property from 1822 to 1837.

552. George Croghan (1791–1849) was an army officer who served as inspector general of the US Army. It's possible that Croghan leased the property from Smith since no deed record appears to substantiate his ownership. Capt. William M. Boyce (1801–55) was a graduate of the US Military Academy in the class of 1822 and served on topographic duty with the US Army and then resigned from the army in 1836 to work on the Geodetic Survey of the Atlantic Coast of the United States. Boyce named the property Montrose due to his ancestral ties with the earls of Montrose. In 1840 Boyce's daughter Jane married Britannia's brother George Washington Peter at Montrose, although Britannia later recalled to her grandson Armistead Peter Jr. that no members of the Peter family attended the wedding because her mother, Martha Peter, didn't approve of the match.

553. Vincent J. Taylor (1812–58) was a partner with Boyce in the operation of Taylor's Mill, which opened in 1836 and was the first flour mill built in Georgetown. It was located on the north side of Water Street (present day K Street NW) near Aqueduct Street, according to the 1853 [Hunter] *Washington and Georgetown Directory*.

554. Mary McEuen Boyce (1804–79) married William Boyce in Philadelphia on February 19, 1829. It was actually Mrs. Boyce, not her husband, who purchased this property from Clement Smith in 1837.

Undated, Williams Place

Old Mrs. Williams the mother owned the square.[555] Gave that piece to her son Brooke.[556] Gave part with Cissel house to her dau[ghter] Mrs. Johns & the homestead—Daniel house she gave to her daughter Mrs. Harry.[557]

555. Harriet Beall (1769–1843) married Elisha "Eli" Owen Williams (1763–1805) in 1784. Mrs. Williams inherited the western portion of this square from her father, Brooke Beall (1742–96). The land was originally part of the large "Rock of Dumbarton" grant of seven hundred acres received by Ninian Beall that was further subdivided among his descendants. Mrs. Williams was widowed about a month after she received the property.

556. Brooke Williams (1790–1843) was the son of Elisha "Eli" Williams and Harriet Beall Williams.

557. The house, now known as the Williams-Addison House, was constructed by Harriet's son-in-law and daughter, Margaret Williams Johns (ca. 1805–post-1854) around 1817. The house is located directly across 31st Street from Tudor Place. George Washington Cissel (1834–1904) purchased the house in 1886 and was the current owner at the time Britannia recounted this to her grandchildren. See note 518 for information about the Bodiscos residing in this same house. Harriet's daughter Margaret Ann Williams married Leonard H. Johns (1778–1824/1833) in 1801. In 1836

at Blandfield, the Beverley's Essex County, Virginia, plantation.

George Croghan (1791–1849). US officer who also served as inspector general of the US Army. He resided in Georgetown and likely leased the Montrose estate from Clement Smith.

George Freeland Peter (1875–1953). Also known as G. Freeland, Freeland. BWPK's youngest grandson and the fourth son born to Dr. and Mrs. Armistead Peter. Freeland was an Episcopal priest who served churches in Washington, DC; Wheeling, West Virginia; and Richmond, Virginia. From 1928 until 1936, Rev. Dr. Peter was a canon of the Washington National Cathedral.

George Lyttleton Upshur (1856–1938). BWPK's great-nephew. George was the son of Katherine Alicia Williams Upshur and John H. Upshur. Unlike his brother, he was not born at TP but rather at the Washington Naval Yard.

George Peter (1779–1861). Also known as Major George Peter, Uncle George. BWPK's paternal uncle. Maj. George Peter served with distinction in the US Army and later commanded a regiment of the Maryland volunteers during the War of 1812. He was elected as a Federalist to the US House of Representatives where he represented Maryland in the Fourteenth and Fifteenth Congresses from 1816 to 1819. After serving in the Maryland House of Delegates from 1819 to 1823, he returned to Congress as a Jacksonian Democrat in the Nineteenth Congress from 1825 to 1827. In addition to a residence in Georgetown, he owned Montanverd, an estate in Montgomery County, Maryland. In 1867 his son Dr. Armistead Peter married BWPK's daughter, Martha "Markie" Custis Kennon.

George Peter Jr. (1829–93). Also known as George. BWPK's first cousin, George was the son of Maj. George Peter and

Sarah "Sallie" Freeland Peter. He was also the brother of Dr. Armistead Peter and Walter Gibson "Gip" Peter.

George Terry Sinclair (1816–85). Also known as Terry Sinclair. The nephew of BWPK's husband, Beverley Kennon, and a member of the wedding party for their 1842 wedding. Sinclair was a native of Norfolk, Virginia, and officer in the US Navy until he resigned his commission to join the Confederate Navy in April 1861. BWPK and her daughter stayed with Sinclair for a week in late November 1861 while they were in Norfolk during the Civil War, and he met with General Huger to arrange passage for BWPK to sail from Norfolk to Baltimore.

George Ticknor (1791–1871). A scholar, bibliophile, and Harvard professor who visited TP on February 19, 1815, describing the event in his diary.

George W. F. Howard Carlisle (1802–64). Also known as Lord Morpeth. A British nobleman whom BWPK met at Daniel Webster's house. He was a member of Parliament and later the seventh earl of Carlisle, Knight of the Garter, and Privy councilor to Queen Victoria. Styled Viscount Morpeth from 1825 to 1848, he visited Washington, DC, as part of his 1842 tour of the United States.

George Washington (1732–99). Also known as General Washington. The step-grandfather of BWPK's mother, Martha Custis Peter. Commander in chief of the Continental Army and later president of the United States from 1789 to 1797. Several sections of the Reminiscences include memories of General Washington passed down to BWPK from her mother, Martha Custis Peter.

George Washington Parke Custis (1781–1857). Also known as Uncle Custis. BWPK's uncle and the only surviving son of John Parke Custis and Eleanor Calvert Custis Stuart. He and his sister, Nelly, became the adopted children of George and Martha Washington and accompanied them to New York and Philadelphia. He built Arlington House on property he inherited from his father. In 1804 he married Mary "Molly" Fitzhugh.

George Washington Peter (1801–77). Also known as Brother Washington, Washington. BWPK's brother. G. W. Peter was the second son born to Thomas and Martha Peter. He married Jane Boyce of Georgetown in 1840. He advised BWPK on business matters and financial decisions from the time of her 1844 widowhood until his death in 1877.

Gertrude/Getty, Sister: see Ann Gertrude Wightt

Gilberta Sinclair Whittle (1824–1906). Niece of Beverley Kennon who was a member of the wedding party when he and BWPK were married on December 8, 1842.

Hannah Pope (1829–1910). The daughter of BWPK's enslaved maid Barbara Cole and a white father who was likely one of the sons of Thomas and Martha Peter. Hannah was a household slave and part of the dowry that BWPK brought to her 1842 marriage to Beverley Kennon. She returned to TP with BWPK in 1844 after Kennon's death. Hannah was sold to Col. John Carter in 1847 because she and his slave Alfred Pope wished to marry. Alfred and Hannah were both manumitted by Carter's will in 1850 and remained in Georgetown for the rest of their lives.

Harrie Webster (1843–1921). Also known as Mr. Webster. The husband of Georgetown neighbor Mary Simpson Hein Webster.

Harriet Beall Williams (1769–1843). Also known as Old Misses Williams. Owner of the square of property located to the east of TP in Georgetown. Through her father, she was a direct descendant of Ninian Beall, the original recipient of the 795-acre land grant comprising nearly all of Georgetown. Her daughter Harriet Beall Williams (1824–90) married the Russian ambassador Aleksandr de Bodisco in 1840.

Harriet Beall Williams de Bodisco Scott (1824–90). Also known as Mrs. Bodisco. A Georgetown schoolgirl who married Russian ambassador Aleksandr de Bodisco when she was sixteen years old. They had six children together before his death in 1854. Seven years later she married Capt. Douglas Scott, a British army officer she met during a tour of India.

Harriet Eugenia Calvert Tuberville Stuart Cazenove (1823–96). Also known as Harriet Stuart. BWPK's distant cousin and a member of the wedding party when she married Beverley Kennon in 1842. Harriet was the daughter of Charles Calvert Stuart, half-brother of BWPK's mother, Martha Custis Peter. Harriet married Louis Sebert "Albert" Cazenove in 1850.

Harriet Williams Harry (1796–1849). Also known as Mrs. Harry. The daughter of Harriet Beall Williams, she inherited land from her mother that was across Congress Street (now 31st street) from the TP property.

Helen Dunlop Laird (1803–32). BWPK's first cousin, the daughter of James and Elizabeth Peter Dunlop. She married William Laird, son of John Laird. She was also the mother of William Laird Jr.

Helen Olivia Lowry Peter (1869–1917). Also known as Cousin Lizzie Lowry. The wife of BWPK's first cousin once removed Robert B. Peter. She briefly lived at TP with BWPK after Dr. Peter and his family moved from TP to their house on O Street in 1882.

Helen Marie Simpson Lueber (1807–90). Also known as Miss Helen Simpson. Gave BWPK piano lessons. Helen married Francis Lueber, an Austrian immigrant who was a merchant in Frederick, Maryland, in 1828. After his death in 1852 Helen moved from Frederick back to Georgetown. Her brother was the Georgetown artist James Alexander Simpson.

Henrietta Johnson Dunlop (1813–93). Also known as Henrietta Dunlop. BWPK's first cousin who was also part of the class that received dancing instruction from Pierre Landrin Duport at TP. Like BWPK, Henrietta attended the Young Ladies Academy at Georgetown's Visitation Convent.

Henrietta Marie Webster Skipwith (1878–1964). A young woman who lived in Georgetown and was close in age to BWPK's grandchildren, especially her granddaughter Agnes.

Henry (unknown life dates). Enslaved coachman and waiter in BWPK's household, 1842–44, at the Washington Navy Yard and later on H Street. He was hired out by BWPK following Commodore Kennon's death in 1844.

Henry Codman Potter (1834–1908). Episcopal minister who served as the seventh bishop of the Episcopal Diocese of New York. He graduated from the Virginia Theological Seminary in Alexandria, Virginia, in 1857.

Henry David Cooke (1825–81). Also known as Henry D. Cooke. A later owner of the Georgetown property known as Carolina Place, Cook purchased the property from O'Neal in 1857. He was a partner in the financial firm Jay Cooke & Co, running the Washington office, and in 1862 he became president of the Washington and Georgetown Street Railway Company. President Ulysses S. Grant appointed Cooke to be the first territorial governor of the District of Columbia, an office he held from 1871 to 1873.

Henry Dunlop (1799–1877). Also known as Cousin Henry. BWPK's first cousin, the son of James Dunlop and Elizabeth Peter Dunlop. BWPK recalled his 1834 marriage to Catherine "Kittee" Louis Ann Thomas.

Henry Howell Lewis (1817–93). Husband of Ann Ogle Tayloe Lewis. It was at a reception held for their 1840 marriage that BWPK was first introduced to her future husband, Beverley Kennon. Through his grandfather Fielding Lewis, he was a great-grand-nephew of George Washington.

Henry Sidney Coxe (1798–1850). Also known as Mr. Coxe. The first husband of Mary Ann Pendleton. They married in 1837, and he died in 1850. Born in Philadelphia, he was the son of Tench and Rebecca Coxe. He was the cashier of the Branch Bank of the United States in St. Louis, Missouri.

Ibby (unknown life dates). Also known as Gran Ibby. An enslaved woman whom BWPK noted as residing at Effingham, a small agricultural property that Thomas Peter owned in northeast Washington, DC. Ibby was a Custis dower slave and the mother of the Peter family's coachman Will Johnson.

Ida Pendleton (1860–1937). A daughter of Mr. and Mrs. William Armistead Pendleton, she lived at TP when her parents rented the property from BWPK, 1858–61.

Isaac Roberdeau (1763–1829). Surveyor, cartographer, and head of the US Army's Topographical Bureau. He resided in Georgetown with his wife, Susan Shippen Blair Roberdeau. BWPK stated that he attended the party held at TP in October 1824 where Lafayette was the guest of honor.

Isabella Wright (unknown life dates). Instructor and headmistress of the school that BWPK attended as a young girl between 1823 and 1825. The school, located on Georgetown's First Street (now N Street) in one of the buildings along Smith's Row, was run by Ms. Wright and her sister Mary.

Jack Gray (unknown life dates). Also known as Little Jack Gray. The son of the Peter family's enslaved seamstress Annie Gray, who resided in a building on a corner of the TP property.

Jacob Asbury Regester (1852–1916). Also known as Reverend Dr. Regester. Episcopal minister who served as rector of St. Paul's church in Buffalo, New York. BWPK first met Dr. Regester during her 1893 trip to Buffalo to visit the grave of her sister America P. Williams, and then he later called at TP during a trip to Washington.

James Bradshaw Beverley (1797–1853). Also known as Bradshaw Beverley, son of Georgetown neighbor Robert Beverley, who owned the Acrolophos estate, now known as Dumbarton Oaks. James was the primary resident of Acrolophos from 1815 until 1823. He married BWPK's first cousin Jane Johns Peter in 1819.

James Dunlop (1755–1823). BWPK's uncle. He married her aunt Elizabeth Peter in 1787. Born in Scotland as heir to the Barony of Garnkirk, he immigrated to the American colonies arriving in New York in 1771 and moved to Georgetown in 1783. In 1792 he purchased Hayes Manor in Montgomery County, Maryland, an estate that would remain in the Dunlop family until 1961.

James Dunlop Jr. (1793–1872). BWPK's first cousin, the son of James and Elizabeth Peter Dunlop. An attorney and later a judge on the Criminal Court of the District of Columbia, Dunlop later served as chief justice of the Circuit Court of the District of Columbia until the court was abolished in 1863.

James Monroe (1758–1836). President of the United States from 1817 to 1836. In 1824 President Monroe invited Lafayette to return to the United States on a yearlong goodwill tour.

Jane Johns Peter Beverley (1800–1863). BWPK's first cousin, she was the daughter of David Peter and his wife, Sarah Johns Peter. Jane married James Bradshaw Beverley in 1819 and resided with him on the Acrolophos estate, now Dumbarton Oaks, until he sold that property in 1823.

Jane Schaaff Johns (?–1854). Also known as Margaretta Jane, Mrs. Johns. The daughter of Dr. John T. Schaaff of Georgetown, she married Bishop John Johns, the fourth Episcopal Bishop of Virginia and later president of the College of William and Mary.

Jane Tayloe Beverley (1774–1816). Also known as Mrs. Beverley. The wife of Robert Beverley. They owned the Acrolophos estate located across Road Street

from TP, now known as Dumbarton Oaks, from 1805 to 1823.

Jared Sparks (1789–1866). Historian and author, later president of Harvard University. Sparks was given access to the Peter family collection of George Washington's papers for his series of edited volumes, *The Writings of George Washington*. Sparks first visited TP in 1828 and wrote about the visit in his diary.

Jean Auguste Marie Chevillié (1765–1837). Also known as John Augustus Chevalier, Mr. Chevalier. A French citizen born in Rochefort who came to Richmond, Virginia, in 1781 while attempting to settle a claim against the Commonwealth of Virginia for munitions supplied during the American Revolution. He remained in Richmond for over twenty years, where he married and engaged in various business ventures.

Jo (unknown life dates). Enslaved individual at TP. BWPK recalled him talking to her mother, Martha Custis Peter, about the time George Washington's tobacco barn caught fire, so it's possible that he was a Custis dower slave who formerly resided at Mount Vernon.

Joanna Prince (unknown life dates). Also known as Miss Joanna; the housekeeper in BWPK's household following her marriage at the Washington Navy Yard. She was likely a white domestic servant as she was always referred to as "Miss Joanna," while the enslaved individuals in the household were only called by their first names.

John Adlum Barber (1838–1905). Also known as Mr. Barber, a resident of Georgetown, the son of Cornelius and Margaret Adlum Barber. He survived the cholera epidemic of 1849 that claimed all four of his sisters.

John Caldwell Calhoun (1782–1850). Also known as John C. Calhoun. A senator from South Carolina who served as secretary of war during President James Monroe's administration from 1817 to 1825. He later served as vice president of the United States from 1825 to 1832, resigning

Marcia Burnes Van Ness (1782–1832). Also known as Mrs. Van Ness. The wife of Maj. Gen. John P. Van Ness and daughter of David Burnes. As BWPK recounted, Van Ness was also the cousin of Ann Gertrude Wightt, the former nun who left Visitation Convent in 1832.

Marcia Helen Middleton (1823–23). Newborn daughter of Arthur Middleton and Ann Van Ness who died, along with her mother, the day after her birth. Both were interred in a neoclassical mausoleum that General Van Ness had constructed in the family cemetery and that was later moved to Georgetown's Oak Hill Cemetery in 1874.

Marcia Van Deventer Stevens (unknown life dates). The daughter of Maj. Christopher Van Deventer and his first wife, Marcia Kellogg Van Deventer. She married Eugene Stevens.

Marcia Van Ness Ouseley (1807–81). Also known as Miss Vann Ness. The niece of Gen. John P. Van Ness who married a British diplomat, Sir William Gore Ouseley, in 1827.

Margaret Ann Williams Johns (ca. 1805–aft. 1854). Also known as Mrs. Johns. The daughter of Harriet Beall Williams. She married Leonard H. Johns in 1801. They owned the house and property across Congress (now 31st) Street from TP.

Margaret Laird (1797–1858). Daughter of Mary Dick Laird and John Laird. She never married and inherited her father's house on N Street, where she lived with her unmarried aunt.

Margaret Peter Dick (1776–1859). Also known as Aunt Dick, BWPK's aunt. She was widowed in 1803 after her husband Robert Dick died on board ship and was buried at sea. After his death she and her young son moved to Georgetown. During BWPK's childhood Margaret lived in Georgetown with her widowed mother, Elizabeth Scott Peter.

Margaret Williams (ca. 1832–33). Also known as Little Margaret. BWPK's niece who died in infancy, one of the children of American P. Peter Williams and William G. Williams.

Maria Beverley Clarke (1791–aft. 1860). Also known as Maria, Mrs. Clarke. Daughter of neighbor Robert Beverley of the Acrolophos estate, located across Road (now R) Street from TP. Mrs. Clarke was also a second cousin of BWPK's husband, Beverley Kennon. BWPK recalled that Mrs. Clarke accompanied her and her mother, Martha Custis Peter, to the reception at the Octagon House where she first met Beverley Kennon in 1841.

Maria Isous de Iturbide (1818–49). Also known as Isous. The daughter of Emperor Augustin I of Mexico and his consort, Anna Maria, she entered the Young Ladies Academy at Georgetown's Visitation Convent in 1826.

Maria von Born Rivardi (?–1830). Also known as Madame Rivardi. The headmistress of the Philadelphia school attended by BWPK's eldest sister, Columbia Washington Peter, between 1811 and 1814. Born in Austria, the daughter of a renowned scientist, she married an Austrian military officer and then immigrated with him to the Caribbean and later the United States where they settled in Philadelphia by 1793. After her husband was given a commission in the US Army, they lived at several frontier forts. They returned to Philadelphia and opened the school in 1802. She was widowed the following year after his death.

Markie. See Martha Custis Kennon Peter; Martha Custis Williams Carter.

Marshall Oliver (1844–1900); professor of mathematics and later librarian of the United States Naval Academy. He married Fanny McTier Smith in 1874.

Martha Custis Kennon Peter (1843–86). Also known as Your Mother, M. C. Kennon Peter, Markie. BWPK's only daughter, born at TP on October 18, 1843. Markie was only four months old when her father, Beverley Kennon, was killed on board the USS *Princeton* in February 1844. She was educated locally in Georgetown and later at schools in Catonsville, Maryland, and Philadelphia. In 1867 she married her first cousin once removed Dr. Armistead Peter. The couple eventually had five children before her death in 1886.

Martha Custis Williams Carter (1827–99). Also known as Martha Carter, Markie. BWPK's niece. The eldest daughter of W. G. Williams and America Peter Williams, Markie came to live at TP after the death of her mother in 1842. She also lived at Arlington House and acted as companion for her widower great-uncle G. W. P. Custis for several years until his death in 1853. In 1877, she married Samuel P. Carter.

Martha Dandridge Custis Washington (1731–1802). Also known as Grandmama Washington; Mrs. Washington. The great-grandmother of BWPK and wife of George Washington. Her first husband, Daniel Parke Custis, whom she married in 1750, died in 1757. Two years later, as a widow with two young children, she married George Washington. When she died in 1802, BWPK's father, Thomas Peter, acted as one of the executors of her estate. Thomas and Martha Peter also attended the sale in July 1802, where they purchased numerous objects formerly owned by George and Martha Washington that they used and displayed at TP.

Martha Eliza Eleanor Peter (1796–1800). Also known as Little Martha, Martha Peter. The first child born to Thomas and Martha Peter in 1796, Martha Washington's first great-grandchild. BWPK said that her mother, Martha Peter, recalled that General Washington and the little girl would walk up and down the portico at Mount Vernon. When she died unexpectedly in 1800, her coffin was placed atop Washington's in the Old Tomb at Mount Vernon.

Martha Parke Custis Peter (1777–1854). Also known as Mother, Patsy, Martha Custis. BWPK's mother, the second daughter of John Parke Custis and Eleanor Calvert Custis. Martha was born in the "blue room" at Mount Vernon on December 31, 1777. She married Thomas Peter in 1795, and they eventually had ten children, five of whom survived to adulthood. Following her death in 1854, BWPK received the TP property per the terms of her will.

Martha "Patsy" Parke Custis (1756–73). The only surviving daughter of Martha Washington from her first marriage to Daniel Parke Custis. She passed away following an epileptic seizure at Mount Vernon in 1773.

Martha "Patty" Washington Dandridge Halyburton (1764–1859). Also known as Patty Halyburton. BWPK's first cousin once removed and a niece of Martha Washington. BWPK discussed with her grandchildren the watch given by Martha Washington to M.W.D. Halyburton.

Martin Van Buren (1782–1862). Also known as Mr. Van Buren. Served as a US senator from New York from 1821 until 1828 and as president of the United States from 1827 to 1841. BWPK recalled that when he was a young senator, his carriage got stuck in the mud when attempting to climb the hill on Congress Street (now 31st Street) in Georgetown on the way to TP.

Mary Ann (unknown life dates). Enslaved woman with unknown role at TP who had a young daughter. After Martha Peter's death in 1854, BWPK allowed Mary Ann to select another master. She ended up in Georgia and later corresponded with BWPK, expressing her desire to make the buckwheat cakes she used to make for her, suggesting that Mary Ann had some degree of literacy.

Mary Ann Berry Coxe Pendleton (1827–90). Also known as Mrs. Pendleton. Wife of William Armistead Pendleton, who with his family rented TP from BWPK from 1858 until late 1861. She was the daughter of Maj. Taylor Berry of St. Louis, Missouri. Her first husband, Henry S. Coxe, was the cashier of the Branch Bank of the United States in St. Louis. She married William A. Pendleton in 1853.

Mary Ann Byrd Kennon (1807–59). Also known as Mary Ann Kennon. The widowed sister-in-law of BWPK's husband, Beverley Kennon. Her husband, Dr. Richard Kennon, died in 1840. She was also the granddaughter of William Byrd III of Virginia's Westover Plantation.

Mary Ann Mason Anderson (1834–1928). Also known as Mrs. Anderson. The eldest daughter of diplomat John Y. Mason. She married Archer Anderson in France in 1859 while her father was serving as US minister plenipotentiary in France. BWPK mentioned that Ann G. Wightt was visiting Mrs. Anderson when she died suddenly in 1867.

Mary Anna Randolph Custis Lee (1807–73). Also known as Cousin Mary, Mary Lee. BWPK's first cousin, the only surviving child of George Washington Parke Custis and Mary Lee Fitzhugh Custis. She married Robert E. Lee at Arlington House in 1831, and BWPK served as a member of the wedding party.

Mary Athenia Forsyth Schaaff (1820–65). Also known as Mary Schaaff. Daughter of Secretary of State John Forsyth, she married Arthur Schaaff of Georgetown in 1824.

Mary Chandler (unknown life dates). A member of the wedding party when BWPK married Beverley Kennon on December 8, 1842, in the TP drawing room. She was the daughter of Maj. Walter Story Chandler and Mary Rogers Chandler of Georgetown and sister of William Chandler.

Mary Dick Laird (unknown life dates). Also known as Miss Dick. The wife of John Laird. They married in 1797. Laird's first wife was Mary's sister Lucinda Dick Laird.

Mary Eliza Angela Lewis Conrad (1813–39). Also known as Angela Lewis, Angela Lewis Conrad. BWPK's first cousin and the daughter of Eleanor "Nelly" Parke Custis Lewis and her husband Lawrence Lewis. In 1835 she married Charles Magill Conrad in Orleans Parish, Louisiana.

Mary Helen Pierce Grant (1837–1927). Also known as Mrs. Grant. The wife of Gen. Lewis Addison Grant. General and Mrs. Grant were among BWPK's tenants at TP after she took in boarders during the Civil War.

Mary Lee "Molly" Fitzhugh Custis (1788–1853). BWPK's aunt. She married George Washington Parke Custis in 1804. She was the mother of Mary Anna Custis Lee.

Mary Lloyd Key Nevins (1801–34). Also known as Mary Key. The eldest daughter of Philip Barton Key. She married Rev. William R. Nevins in 1822.

Mary McEuen Boyce (1804–79). Also known as Miss McEwen. Wife of Capt. William M. Boyce of a neighboring Georgetown estate, Montrose. Her daughter Jane Boyce was BWPK's sister-in-law.

Mary Pendleton (1857–92). A daughter of Mr. and Mrs. William Armistead Pendleton, she lived at TP when her parents rented the property from BWPK, 1858–61.

Mary Schaaff Stevenson (1820–65). Daughter of Dr. John T. Schaaff and his first wife, Mary Sydebothan Schaaff. She married Andrew Stevenson, US minister to the United Kingdom. Following Stevenson's death in 1857, Mary returned to Georgetown and resided with her unmarried sister. During the Civil War, Mary and her sister Ann were in Staunton, Virginia, with BWPK and Markie per a Lee family letter from May 1861.

Mary Stewart Schaaff (1773–1860). Also known as Mrs. Schaaff. The second wife of Dr. John T. Schaaff of Georgetown.

Mary Sydebothan Schaaff (1776–1810). First wife of Dr. John T. Schaaff of Georgetown, mother of the five Schaaff children discussed by BWPK.

Mary Wright (unknown life dates). Also known as Miss Mary. One of two sisters who operated the school on Georgetown's First (Now N) Street that BWPK attended as a young girl from 1823 to 1825. A Mary J. Wright appears on the 1820 US Census as living in Georgetown in the same household as one other white woman between the ages of twenty-six and forty-five years old, likely her sister Isabella.

Nancey (unknown life dates). Enslaved laundress at TP during BWPK's childhood.

Nicholas Power Tillinghast (1817–69). Also known as Mr. Tillinghast, Rev. Tillinghast, Rev. Mr. Tillinghast. Rector of St. John's, Georgetown, from 1848 to 1867. A native of Providence, Rhode Island, he attended Brown University and the Virginia Theological Seminary. BWPK recalled him calling on her at TP and asking her to remove a boxwood cross she had made and attached to the pulpit of St. John's Church as an Easter decoration.

Patty Allen (unknown life dates). Also known as Patty, Old Patty. The enslaved cook at TP during BWPK's childhood. She lived off property with her free husband and attended Christ Episcopal Church in Georgetown, where she appears on a ca. 1820–30 list of "Communicants among the Coloured People."

Peregrine Warfield (1779–1856). A Georgetown physician who was called to TP to amputate the leg of Thomas Peter's enslaved valet Charlie in 1824. He was also a founder of the Medical Society of the District of Columbia.

Philip Barton Key (1757–1815). Judge appointed to the Fourth United States Circuit Court in 1801 by President John Adams, serving until the court was abolished in 1802. He later won election as a congressman from Maryland from 1807 to 1813. He resided in Georgetown with his daughters, whom BWPK recalled.

Philip Barton Key II (1818–59). Son of Francis Scott Key, US attorney for the District of Columbia, and murder victim. He was shot and killed by Congressman Daniel Sickles after it was revealed that he was carrying on an affair with Sickles's wife.

Philip Rogers Hoffman (1806–73). Also known as Mr. Hoffman. The husband of Emily Louise Key and son-in-law of Philip Barton Key. He was from Baltimore, Maryland.

Phillips Brooks (1825–93). The longtime rector of Trinity Church, Boston, and lyricist of the popular Christmas hymn "Oh, Little Town of Bethlehem." Brooks graduated from the Virginia Theological Seminary in 1859.

Pierre Landrin Duport (1762–1841). Also known as Mr. DuPort. A dancing instructor in Georgetown from whom BWPK took dancing lessons. DuPort claimed that he had taught the children of Marie Antoinette before fleeing France. He arrived in Philadelphia in 1790 and was in Georgetown by 1812. He came to TP and provided instruction for BWPK and other young ladies in the neighborhood.

Rebecca Ann Key Howard Tyson (1809–89). Also known as Rebecca Key. A daughter of Philip Barton Key who attended school with BWPK at the Young Ladies Academy, although she was several years older. She married Dr. William Howard of Baltimore in 1828. Following his death, she married Dr. Alexander H. Tyson of Baltimore in 1837.

Rebecca Beck Williams (1804–80). Also known as Miss Beck. The wife of Brooke Williams Sr. who lived on a neighboring property in Georgetown.

Reuel Keith (1792–1842). Also known as Rev. Keith. Episcopal minister who served as rector of Christ Church in Georgetown from 1817 to 1820. He later served as president of the Virginia Theological Seminary in Alexandria. While in that role, he officiated the wedding of Robert E. Lee and Mary Anna Custis in 1831. BWPK recalled a humorous episode from the Lee wedding where Reverend Keith, after getting drenched in a summer thunderstorm, had to wear a pair of her uncle G.W.P. Custis's trousers to perform the marriage ceremony.

Richard Edward Hazzard (1804–31). A friend and fellow army officer of BWPK's brother-in-law, William G. Williams. As BWPK recalled, Hazzard was jilted by Rebecca Key. Williams painted a portrait of Hazzard that is now in the TP collection.

Richard Parrot (1766–1823). Also known as Mr. Parrot. A Georgetown industrialist who owned a ropewalk and a mill. The ropewalk was burned by the British in 1814. Parrot owned an estate in upper Georgetown located on Road Street that he named Elderslie. It was renamed Montrose by later owners. It is now the location of Montrose Park in Georgetown.

Robert B. Peter (1868–1936). Judge and attorney. BWPK's first cousin once removed. He was a son of George Peter Jr. and a grandson of Maj. George Peter.

Robert Beverley (1769–1843). A neighbor in Georgetown. In 1805 Beverley purchased the Rock of Dumbarton estate from W. H. Dorsey, across Road Street from TP, re-naming it Acrolophos, now known as Dumbarton Oaks. Beverley served as president of Georgetown's Union Bank from 1809 to 1811 and also operated a shipping business until the War of 1812 when he returned to Blandfield, his Essex County, Virginia, plantation.

Robert Dick (1800–1870). Also known as Cousin Robert Dick. BWPK's first cousin, the only son of Margaret Peter Dick and Thomas Dick. As BWPK recalled, in 1861 while she was away from Georgetown, he helped move her furniture and possessions from storage at the Seminary Building to another location after it was seized by the federal government for use as a hospital during the Civil War.

Robert Dunlop (1795–1869). Also known as Cousin Robert Dunlop. BWPK's first cousin, the son of James Dunlop and Elizabeth Peter Dunlop.

Robert E. Lee (1807–70). Also known as Cousin Robert, Gen. Lee. Husband of BWPK's first cousin, Mary Anna Custis Lee. BWPK served as a member of the wedding party for their 1831 marriage. Lee eventually commanded the Confederate Army during the Civil War and later served as president of Washington College. BWPK recalled that Lee always called her "Cousin Britt."

Robert Edge Pine (1730–88). English painter who settled in Philadelphia in 1784. He visited Mount Vernon in 1785, hoping to paint a portrait of George Washington, and during the visit painted portraits of Martha Washington's four Custis grandchildren. The portrait of Martha Parke Custis Peter was at TP until her death in 1854 when it descended to BWPK's brother G. W. Peter. As BWPK recalled, this was the only time her mother ever sat for a portrait.

Robert Peter (1726–1806). Also known as Grandpa Peter. BWPK's paternal grandfather. Born near Lanarkshire, Scotland, he immigrated to the Maryland colony by 1746, first residing in Bladensburg and eventually settling in Georgetown in 1752, where he opened a store and acted as the purchasing agent for the Scottish tobacco firm of John Glassford & Company. In 1797 he served as the first mayor of Georgetown. At the time of his death in 1806 he owned more than twenty thousand acres of land.

Robert Thomas Peter (1806–7). Brother of BWPK who died in infancy.

Roberta Beverley Lightfoot (?–1834). Daughter of Robert Beverley and Jane Tayloe Beverley. She lived at Acrolophos, now Dumbarton Oaks, adjacent to TP, during BWPK's childhood. She died several months after marrying William Bernard Lightfoot.

Rosalie Eugenia Calvert Carter (1806–45). BWPK's first cousin once removed, the daughter of Rosalie Stier

Calvert and George Calvert of Riversdale. In 1830 she married Charles Henry Carter.

Rosalie Stier Calvert (1778–1821). A great-aunt of BWPK. She was the husband of George Calvert, and they resided at Riversdale in Prince George's County, Maryland. BWPK's mother, Martha Parke Custis Peter, stayed at Riversdale to run the household for two months during Rosalie's final illness in 1821. BWPK was close in age to several of Rosalie's children who are mentioned in the Reminiscences.

Sabina María de la Concepción de Iturbide (1810–71). Also known as Sabina. One of the daughters of the former emperor of Mexico, Augustin I, and his wife, Anna Maria. Sabina and her sisters entered the Young Ladies Academy at Georgetown's Visitation Convent in July of 1826.

Sall Twine (ca. 1761–aft. 1802). A Custis dower slave who was a field laborer at George Washington's Dogue Run Farm. She was among the enslaved individuals inherited by Thomas and Martha Peter after Martha Washington's death in 1802. Sall had seven children with her husband George, a slave at Washington's Mansion House Farm, including a daughter Barbara, also known as Barbary, who later served as BWPK's lady's maid at TP.

Sarah (unknown life dates). Enslaved chambermaid in BWPK's household at the Navy Yard and later on H Street from 1842 to 1844.

Sarah Elizabeth Peter Slaymaker (1831–90). Also known as Cousin Sarah Elizabeth Slaymaker. BWPK's first cousin, the eldest daughter of John Parke Custis Peter and his wife, Elizabeth Jane Henderson. She was born at TP on February 11, 1831.

Sarah Jane Wingfield Williams (1775–aft. 1861). Mother of BWPK's brother-in-law, William G. Williams. She was born in Georgia and married William Williams Sr. of Gravesend, England, at Philadelphia's Christ Church

on January 5, 1797. Both of her children were born in the United States between 1799 and 1801, after which she and her husband returned to England.

Sarah Johns Peter (1777–1823). BWPK's aunt. She married David Peter on September 17, 1799. They resided at Peter Grove, a property on Road (now R) Street several blocks from TP.

Sarah "Sallie" Freeland Peter (1805–46). Also known as Aunt Sallie. BWPK's aunt, the third wife of her uncle George Peter and younger sister of his second wife, Agnes Freeland Peter.

Stacia (?–ca. 1892). Enslaved maid and nurse/nanny at TP, sister of Brythe and Elizabeth. She nursed BWPK's nephew Orton through his bout with typhoid fever in 1847. Following her emancipation, Stacia remained in Georgetown, and BWPK would send her small financial gifts. The last recorded gift is in October 1892.

Thomas Dick (1773–1803). BWPK's uncle. He married Margaret Peter in 1798. He died on board ship on a trip to the West Indies in 1803 and was buried at sea. As BWPK recounted, two of his sisters were the wives of John Laird.

Thomas Henderson (1789–1854). A physician who practiced medicine in Georgetown from 1816 to 1826, when he moved his practice to downtown Washington. He was also a professor of medicine at the Columbian Medical College.

Thomas Jefferson (1743–1826). President of the United States, 1801–9, and author of the Declaration of Independence. BWPK alludes to Jefferson's politics and his role as one of the founders of the Democratic-Republican political party. In 1908 BWPK stated that she considered herself a "Federalist of '76'" and that her political beliefs were closely allied with those of her parents, who opposed not only Jefferson but also the Democratic-Republicans who followed him as president—James Madison and James Monroe.

Thomas Law (1756–1834). Also known as Mr. Law. BWPK's uncle. Born in England, Law worked as an agent for the East India Company for eighteen years before returning to England for his health. He immigrated to the United States in 1794 and married Elizabeth "Eliza" Parke Custis in 1796. Law and Eliza separated in 1804 and divorced in 1811.

Thomas Peter (1769–1834). Also known as Father. BWPK's father. The eldest son of Robert Peter and Elizabeth Scott Peter, Thomas Peter married Martha Parke Custis in January 1795. He purchased the TP property from Frances Lowndes in 1805. In addition to TP, he owned Oakland, a large agricultural estate in Montgomery County, Maryland, and Effingham, a smaller farm in northeastern Washington, DC.

Thomas Sim (1770–1832). A local Georgetown physician who was called to TP to amputate the leg of Thomas Peter's enslaved valet Charlie in 1824 after a carriage accident crushed his leg. Dr. Sim died after contracting cholera after treating patients during the cholera epidemic of 1832.

Thomas Turner (1807–83). A career officer in the US Navy. He married BWPK's friend Frances "Fannie" Palmer in Philadelphia in 1836. BWPK was a bridesmaid in the wedding.

Thomas Whitfoot O'Neal (1812–69). Born in Barbados, he married Ann Eliza Carter, daughter of John Carter of Georgetown in 1842. He was widowed after Ann's death, and their son John Carter O'Neal eventually inherited the property in Georgetown that his grandfather had named Carolina Place. At the time of his death in 1869, T. W. O'Neal was residing at 25 The Circus, Bath, England.

Tobias Lear (1762–1816). Personal secretary of President George Washington from 1784 to 1799. His third wife, Frances "Fanny" Dandridge Henley, was a distant relative of BWPK. Lear committed suicide in 1816.

Ulysses S. Grant (1822–85). Former commanding general of the US Army during the American Civil War and president of the United States from 1869 to 1877. As BWPK described, when Robert E. Lee stayed at TP during his final visit to Washington, DC, he also paid a visit to President Grant at the White House.

Vincent J. Taylor (1812–58). The business partner of William Boyce in the operation of the first flour mill constructed in Georgetown, known as Taylor's Mill.

Virginie Bridon de Greuhm Lawless (1794–1860). Also known as Baroness Greuhm, Virginia de Greuhm Lawless. The wife of Baron de Greuhm, the Prussian minister whom she married in Washington in 1819. Baron de Greuhm died in 1823, and in 1825 she married Luke Lawless, a British lawyer in Georgetown; they later moved to St. Louis, Missouri. BWPK recalled that Baroness de Greuhm presented Martha Custis Peter with a "crystal with medallion head of Washington," likely a sulfide portrait of the president.

Vladimir de Bodisco (1825–78). Also known as Waldemar de Bodisco. A nephew of Baron de Bodisco, the Russian ambassador. Vladimir accompanied his uncle to Georgetown and graduated from Georgetown College in 1848, after which he served as secretary of the Russian Legation in Washington for nearly twenty years. In 1871 he was appointed consul general in New York and served in that position until his death in 1878.

Walter Dulany Addison (1769–1848). Also known as Rev. Mr. Addison. Rector of St. John's Episcopal Church, Georgetown, 1809–21, 1823–27, and 1829–31. In this role he officiated the marriage of BWPK's sister America Pinckney Peter to William G. Williams at TP in 1826.

Walter Gibson Peter (1842–63). Also known as Gip. BWPK's first cousin. A son of Maj. George Peter and his third wife, Sarah "Sallie" Freeland Peter. Gip was a soldier in the Confederate Army and served first with the 8th Virginia Cavalry and then, at the request of his cousin William Orton Williams, was transferred to Gen. Braxton Bragg's corps. Gip and his cousin W. O. Williams were executed as spies near Franklin, Tennessee, on June 9, 1863.

Walter Gibson Peter (1868–1945). Also known as Walter. BWPK's eldest grandson, the first child born to Dr. Armistead Peter and Martha "Markie" Kennon Peter. Walter received a degree in architecture from the Massachusetts Institute of Technology and was a practicing architect in Washington until his death in 1945.

Walter Wheeler Williams (1834–92). Also known as Rev. Mr. Williams. Rector of Christ Episcopal Church, Georgetown from 1866 to 1876. In this appointment, he presided over the marriage of BWPK's daughter Martha "Markie" Kennon to Dr. Armistead Peter at TP in 1868.

Will Johnson (unknown life dates). A Custis dower slave and enslaved coachman at TP during BWPK's childhood, Will also tended the Peter family's smokehouse. As coachman, he took BWPK to school each day, placing her behind him on a horse.

Will Twine (1784–1832). Enslaved gardener at TP who contracted cholera during the 1832 cholera epidemic and died. Although enslaved and owned by Thomas Peter, he lived off site with a free wife in the area of Georgetown known as Lee's Hill.

William Armistead Pendleton (1825–70). Also known as Mr. Pendleton. A lawyer who, with his family, rented TP from BWPK from 1858 to 1861. He was the son of John L. Pendleton and Eliza Bankhead Magruder.

William B. Sinclair (1818–95). Also known as Dr. Sinclair. The nephew of Beverley Kennon who was a member of the wedding party when Kennon and BWPK married at TP on December 8, 1842.

William Bernard Lightfoot (1811–70). Also known as Mr. Lightfoot. Husband of Roberta Beverley Lightfoot.

William Bradshaw Beverley (1791–1866). Son of Robert and Jayne Tayloe Beverley, who were neighbors in Georgetown and owned the Acrolophos property across Road Street from TP between 1805 and 1823, during BWPK's childhood.

William Chandler (1812–92). An officer in the US Navy and member of the wedding party when BWPK married Beverley Kennon at TP on December 8, 1842. He resigned from the US Navy at the outbreak of the Civil War and later served in the British Mercantile Marine. Raised in Georgetown, he was a son of Maj. Walter Story Chandler and Margaret Rogers Chandler. His maternal grandfather was John Rogers, first chancellor of Maryland and a delegate to the Continental Congress.

William Dandridge Kennon (1832–72). Also known as Dan. BWPK's stepson. The youngest son of Beverley Kennon and his first wife, Elizabeth Dandridge Claiborne Kennon. Dan served in the Confederate Army during the Civil War and later as a sailor in the US Revenue Cutter Service.

William Dickinson Hawley (1784–1845). Also known as Rev. Mr. Hawley. The longtime rector of St. John's Church, Lafayette Square, holding the position from 1817 until his death in 1845. BWPK recalled that he conducted her confirmation and that of her older sister America because the rector of Christ Church in Georgetown refused to confirm anyone who did not renounce dancing. BWPK also noted that her daughter, Markie, attended a school in Washington run by two of Rev. Hawley's daughters.

William Frederick Havemeyer II (1850–1913). Also known as Mr. Havemeyer. Son of New York City mayor William F. Havemeyer and a collector of manuscripts and objects associated with George Washington. He was the previous owner of the Edward Savage portrait, *The Washington*

Family, now in the Andrew W. Mellon Collection of the National Gallery of Art.

William G. Williams (1801–46). Also known as Capt. Williams, Lt. Williams. BWPK's brother-in-law. He married America Pinckney Peter at TP on June 27, 1826. An 1824 graduate of the US Military Academy, Williams was an officer in the Topographical Corps. He was killed while leading a charge during the Battle of Monterey in the Mexican-American War in September 1846.

William Henry Kennon (1832–76). Nephew of Beverley Kennon and a member of the wedding party when Kennon married BWPK at TP on December 8, 1842. He also served as Beverley Kennon's clerk at the Navy Department.

William Howard (1794–1834). Baltimore physician who married Rebecca Ann Key, the daughter of Philip Barton Key. He was known for his grand residence in Baltimore, which featured an ornate portico supported by four marble columns.

William J. Clarke (unknown life dates). Also known as Reverend Mr. Clarke. Principal of the Female Academy, Georgetown, the school formerly known as Miss English's school, between 1852 and 1857. During that time, BWPK's daughter, Markie, was a pupil at the school.

William Laird Dunlop (1830–1916). Also known as Cousin William. The son of BWPK's first cousin, Judge James Dunlop. At the time when BWPK recounted many of her memories to her grandchildren, he resided in the house on N Street in Georgetown that was originally built by his grandfather, John Laird.

William Laird Jr. (1828–91). Also known as Mr. Laird Jr. BWPK's first cousin once removed. He was the son of William Laird Sr. and Helen Dunlop Laird.

William Laird Sr. (1800–1874). Also known as Cousin William Laird. He was the son and business partner of tobacco merchant John Laird. Like his father, he was married twice, and his wives were sisters. His wives, Helen Dunlop Laird and Arianna French Dunlop Laird, were BWPK's first cousins.

William M. Boyce (1801–55). Also known as Capt. Boyce. A neighbor in Georgetown who owned the Montrose estate. A graduate of the US Military Academy in the class of 1822, Boyce served on topographic duty with the US Army and then resigned his commission in 1836 to work on the Geodetic Survey of the Atlantic Coast of the United States. In 1840 Boyce's daughter Jane married BWPK's brother George Washington Peter.

William MacPherson Hornor (1860–1937). Also known as Little Mackie Hornor. The son of Dr. and Mrs. Caleb Hornor, who were tenants at TP during the Civil War when BWPK took in boarders.

William Marbury (1762–1835). A Georgetown businessman and plaintiff in the landmark 1803 US Supreme Court Case *Marbury v. Madison*. Outgoing president John Adams made a number of last-minute appointments, including naming Marbury a justice of the peace of the District of Columbia, the day before he left office. Incoming president Thomas Jefferson refused to honor Adams' appointments. Marbury resided in Georgetown.

William Masters Camac (1802–42). Lived at 353 Chestnut Street in Philadelphia. BWPK attended a ball at his house during a ca. 1836 visit to Philadelphia prior to her marriage.

William Matthews (1770–1854). Also known as Old Father Matthews. The first American-born Catholic priest ordained in Washington, DC, by Bishop Carroll in 1800. Matthews served for many years as pastor of Washington's St. Patrick's Catholic Church. In 1809, while retaining his role as pastor of St. Patrick's, he entered the Society of Jesus and succeeded his uncle Francis Neale as president of Georgetown College, a position he held for eight months.

William Mead (1789–1862). Also known as Rev. Mr. Mead. Bishop of Virginia, a cousin of Mrs. G.W.P. Custis who was incorrectly credited with conducting the 1831 wedding of Mr. and Mrs. Robert E. Lee.

William Norwood (1806–87). Also known as Rev. Mr. Norwood. Rector of Christ Church, Georgetown, from 1854 until 1861 during the time BWPK attended the church. He previously served as rector of St. Paul's Episcopal Church in Richmond from 1845 to 1849. BWPK recalled his Southern sympathies during the time just before the Civil War.

William Orton Williams (1842–63). Also known as Orton. BWPK's nephew, the youngest surviving son of America P. Peter Williams and Captain William G. Williams. Orton and his siblings came to TP following their mother's death in the spring of 1842 to be raised by their grandmother Martha Peter. Orton attended Episcopal High School in Alexandria, Virginia, in 1853–54 at Robert E. Lee's recommendation. Lee later arranged for Orton to receive an appointment to Gen. Winfield Scott's staff in the US Army. Orton was imprisoned for a month after he was charged with providing information to Lee's family. Upon his release, he resigned his commission and joined the Confederate Army. He was sent west to serve on the staff of Gen. Leonidas Polk but was later reassigned after killing a man for refusing an order. Orton was later placed on the staff of Gen. Braxton Bragg and rose to the rank of colonel following the Battle of Shiloh. He and his cousin Walter Gibson "Gip" Peter were captured in Franklin, Tennessee, and hanged as spies following a drumhead court-martial on June 9, 1863.

William P. Powell (1834–1915). Also known as Powell. A physician who was hired as a contract assistant surgeon for the Union Army and later worked for a year at the Contraband Hospital, a facility in Washington providing medical care to former slaves.

William Pendleton Jr. (1860–1916). Son of Mr. and Mrs. William Armistead Pendleton, he lived at TP when his parents rented the property from BWPK, 1858–61.

William Shubrick (1796–1857). US naval officer who rose to the rank of rear admiral. BWPK's late husband Cdre. Kennon served as Captain of the *Macedonian*, Admiral Shubrick's flagship in the Caribbean from 1838 to 1840. He paid BWPK $18 in June 1844 for the hiring out of the enslaved cook Charity, who had formerly worked in the Naval Yard and H Street houses. In October he paid BWPK another $27 for hiring out both Charity and her daughter, Fanny.

William Thornton (1759–1828). Also known as Dr. Thornton. A physician and amateur architect who designed TP for Thomas and Martha Peter. He also designed the Octagon House for Col. John Tayloe and first gained recognition as an architect after submitting the winning entry in the competition for the design of the US Capitol Building in 1792.

William White (1748–1836). Also known as Bishop White. The first and fourth presiding bishop of the Episcopal Church of the United States as well as the first bishop of the Diocese of Pennsylvania. BWPK recalled that he presided over a marriage in which she was a member of the wedding party in 1836.

William Williams Sr. (1771–1845). Father of BWPK's brother-in-law, William G. Williams. Born in Gravesend, England, he came to the United States sometime before 1797, the year in which he married Sarah Jane Wingfield at Philadelphia's Christ Church. Both of his children were born in the United States before he and his wife returned to England. He returned to the United States at least once in 1843–44 to visit his son and grandchildren, who were living in Buffalo, New York.

William Wilson Corcoran (1798–1888). Also known as W. W. Corcoran. Philanthropist, banker, and art collector who lived in Washington. As BWPK noted, he was a later owner of the house occupied by Daniel Webster adjacent to Lafayette Square. Corcoran donated the land for Georgetown's Oak Hill Cemetery and also founded the Louise Home, a residence for impoverished Southern widows, of which BWPK served as a longtime directress.

Bibliography

ARCHIVAL SOURCES

Albert and Shirley Small Special Collections Library, University of Virginia, Charlottesville
Peter Family Papers.

Arlington House, Arlington, Virginia
Arlington House Manuscripts.

Cornell University Library, Ithaca, New York
Arthur H. and Mary Marden Dean Lafayette Collection.

Library of Congress (LOC), Washington, DC
Andrew Jackson Papers: Series 1, General Correspondence and Related Items, Manuscript Division.
Thornton, Anna Maria, *Diaries of Mrs. William Thornton*, Anna Maria Brodeau Thornton Papers, Manuscript Division.

Massachusetts Historical Society, Boston
Timothy Pickering Papers.

Mount Vernon Library, Mount Vernon, Virginia
Papers of Britannia W. Peter Kennon, Peter Family Papers.
Papers of Thomas Peter, Peter Family Papers.

National Archives and Records Administration (NARA), College Park, Maryland
"Office of the Provost Marshall, Fort Monroe [Virginia], December 6, 1861." Union Citizens File, NARA, RG 109, Roll 153. Accessed via Fold3.com

Tudor Place Archives (TPA), Washington, DC
Kuniholm, Berthe E. "Transcription of the Diaries of Mrs. William Thornton, 1793–1863." Typescript found in the Research Files, Tudor Place Research Library.
Papers of Armistead Peter 3rd.
Papers of Armistead Peter Jr.
Papers of Beverley Kennon.
Papers of Britannia W. Kennon.
Papers of Dr. Armistead Peter.
Papers of Martha Washington.
Papers of Thomas and Martha Peter.

Virginia Historical Society, Richmond
Lee Family Papers.

PUBLISHED WORKS

Abbot, W. W., ed. *The Papers of George Washington, Revolutionary War Series.* Vol. 1, *June–September 1775*, ed. Philander D. Chase. Charlottesville: University Press of Virginia, 1985.

"Abstracts of Virginia Land Patents." *Virginia Magazine of History and Biography* 1, no. 3 (1894): 310–24.

Adams, Herbert Baxter. *The Life and Writings of Jared Sparks*. Vol. 2. Boston: Houghton Mifflin, 1893.

"The Aged Women's Home of Georgetown." In Report of the Commissioners of the District of Columbia, *Executive Documents Printed by Order of the House of Representatives, 1875–76*. Washington, DC: US GPO, 1876.

Alexander, Robert B. *The Architecture of Baltimore: An Illustrated History*. Baltimore: Johns Hopkins University Press, 2004.

Allen, William C. "An Architectural History of Tudor Place." In *Tudor Place: America's Story Lives Here*. Edited by Leslie L. Buhler. Washington, DC: White House Historical Association, 2016.

American State Papers: Documents, Legislative and Executive, of the Congress of the United States, For the First and Second Sessions of the Twenty-Fourth Congress, Commencing January 12, 1836 and Ending February 25, 1837. Vol. 6, *Military Affairs*. Washington, DC: Gales & Seaton, 1861.

Architrave P.C., Architects; Rhodeside & Harwell, Inc; and Robinson & Associates, Inc. *Montrose Park: Cultural Landscape Report*. Washington, DC: National Park Service, US Department of the Interior, 2004.

"Arlington and Mount Vernon 1856. As Described in a Letter of Augusta Blanche Berard." *Virginia Magazine of History and Biography* 57, no. 2 (1949): 140–75.

Armstrong, William. "Some New Washington Relics, I. From the Collection of Mrs. B. W. Kennon." *Century Monthly Illustrated Magazine* 40, no. 1 (May 1890).

Bailey, Candace. *Charleston Belles Abroad: The Music Collections of Harriet Lowndes, Henrietta Aiken, and Louisa Rebecca McCord*. Columbia: University of South Carolina Press, 2019.

Balch, Thomas Bloomer. *Reminiscences of Georgetown, D.C.: Second Lecture Delivered in the Methodist Protestant Church, Georgetown, DC, March 9, 1859*. Washington, DC: Henry Polkinhorn Printer, 1859.

Bancroft, Hubert Howe. *The Works of Hubert Howe Bancroft*. Vol. 4, *History of Mexico: 1804–1824*. San Francisco: A. L. Bancroft, 1885.

Barnes, Robert W. *Gleanings from Maryland Newspapers*. Vol. 4. Lutherville, MD: B. Carothers, 1975.

"The Battle of Thompsons Station and the Trial of Spies in Franklin, Tennessee." In *United Service: A Monthly Review of Military and Naval Affairs*. Vol. 3. New Series. Philadelphia: L. R. Hamersley, 1890.

Bergheim, Laura. *The Washington Historical Atlas: Who Did What When and Where in the Nation's Capital*. Rockville, MD: Woodbine House, 1992.

Berry, Thomas S. "The Rise of Flour Milling in Richmond." *Virginia Magazine of History and Biography* 78, no. 4 (October 1970): 387–408.

Bierne, Frances F. *The Amiable Baltimoreans*. Baltimore: Johns Hopkins University Press, 1984.

Blackman, Ann. "Fatal Cruise of the Princeton." *Naval History*, October 2005, pp. 37–41.

Bower, Mark Arnold. "Loudoun, Germantown, Philadelphia County House of the Armat Family: The Years 1801–1835." Master's thesis, University of Pennsylvania, 1984.

Brady, Patricia, ed. *George Washington's Beautiful Nelly: The Letters of Eleanor Parke Custis to Elizabeth Bordley Gibson, 1794–1851*. Columbia: University of South Carolina Press, 1991.

Brandt, Nat. *The Congressman Who Got Away with Murder*. Syracuse, NY: Syracuse University Press, 1991.

Browning, Charles Henry. *Americans of Royal Descent: A Collection of Genealogies of American Families Whose Lineage Is Traced to the Legitimate Issue of Kings*. Philadelphia: Porter & Coates, 1891.

Bryan, W. B., ed. "Diary of Mrs. William Thornton. Capture of Washington by the British." In *Records of the Columbia*

Historical Society. Vol. 19. Washington, DC: Columbia Historical Society, 1916.

Brydon, G. MacLaren. "Historic Parishes: St. Paul's Church, Richmond." *Historical Magazine of the Protestant Episcopal Church* 23, vol. 3 (September 1954): 277–92.

Buckley, Cornelius Michael. *Stephen Larigaudelle Dubuisson, S.J. (1786–1864) and the Reform of the American Jesuits.* Lanham, MD: University Press of America, 2013.

Bushong, William. *Historic Resources Study: Rock Creek Park, District of Columbia.* Washington, DC: US Park Service, Department of the Interior, 1990.

Cadou, Carol B. *The George Washington Collection: Fine and Decorative Arts at Mount Vernon.* Mount Vernon Ladies Association. New York: Hudson Hills Press, 2006.

Calcott, Margaret Law. *Mistress of Riversdale: The Plantation Letters of Rosalie Stier Calvert, 1795–1821.* Baltimore: Johns Hopkins University Press, 1993.

Carrier, Thomas J. *Historic Georgetown: A Walking Tour.* Charleston, SC: Arcadia, 1999.

Carusi, Gaetano. *Narrative of Gaetano Carusi, in Support of His Claim before the Congress of the United States.* Washington, DC, 1837. Digitized copy from the collection of the British Library found via GoogleBooks.

Cary, Wilson Miles. "The Dandridges of Virginia." *William and Mary Quarterly* 5, no. 1 (1896): 30–39.

Castle, Guy. "Life in Georgetown, 1819–1841, as Told in the Personal Correspondence of Ann Shaaff." In *Records of the Columbia Historical Society.* Vol. 60/62, pp. 75–83. Washington, DC: Columbia Historical Society, 1960/1962.

Chase, Philander D., ed. *The Papers of George Washington, Revolutionary War Series.* Vol. 1, *16 June 1775–15 September 1775.* Charlottesville: University Press of Virginia, 1985.

Clarke, Allen C. "Doctor and Mrs. William Thornton." In *Records of the Columbia Historical Society.* Vol. 18. Washington, DC: Columbia Historical Society, 1915.

———. "General John Peter Van Ness, a Mayor of the City of Washington, His Wife Marcia, and Her Father David Burnes." In *Records of the Columbia Historical Society*, vol. 22, 125–204. Columbia Historical Society, Washington, DC, 1919.

———. *Life and Letters of Dolly Madison.* Washington, DC: Press of W. F. Roberts Co., 1914.

Cogar, William B. *Dictionary of Admirals of the U.S. Navy.* Vol. 1, *1862–1900.* Annapolis, MD: Naval Institute Press, 1989.

Coles, William B. *The Coles Family of Virginia: Its Numerous Connections, from the Emigration to America to the Year 1915.* New York, 1931.

Coulter, E. Merton. *A History of the South.* Vol. 8, *The South during Reconstruction, 1865–1877.* Baton Rouge: Louisiana State University Press, 1947.

Covey, Herbert C., and Bernard Eisnach. *What the Slaves Ate: Recollections of African American Foods and Foodways from the Slave Narratives.* Santa Barbara, CA: Greenwood, 2009.

Crew, Harvey W. *Centennial History of the City of Washington, D.C.: With Full Outline of the Natural Advantages, Accounts of the Indian Tribes, Selection of the Site, Founding of the City . . . to the Present Time.* Washington, DC: H. W. Crew, 1892.

Cullum, George W. *Biographical Register of the Officers and Graduates of the United States Military Academy at West Point, New York, since Its Establishment in 1802.* Boston: Houghton Mifflin, 1891.

Custis, George Washington Parke, Mary Randolph Custis Lee, and Benson John Lossing. *Recollections and Private Memoirs of Washington by His Adopted Son, George Washington Parke Custis, with a Memoir of the Author by His Daughter.* New York: Derby & Jackson, 1860.

Deas, Alston. "Eleanor Parke Lewis to Mrs. C. C. Pinckney." *South Carolina Historical Magazine* 63, no. 1 (January 1962): 12–17.

Debutts, Mary Custis Lee, ed. *Growing Up in the 1850s: The Journal of Agnes Lee.* Chapel Hill: University of North Carolina Press, 1988.

DeFerrari, John. *Capital Streetcars: Early Mass Transit in Washington, D.C.* Charleston, SC: Arcadia, 2015.

Dixon, Joan M. *National Intelligencer Newspaper Abstracts, 1814–1817.* Westminster, MD: Heritage, 1997.

———. *National Intelligencer Newspaper Abstracts, 1824–1826.* Westminster, MD: Heritage, 1999.

———. *National Intelligencer Newspaper Abstracts, 1842.* Westminster, MD: Heritage, 2004.

———. *National Intelligencer Newspaper Abstracts, 1858.* Westminster, MD: Heritage, 2008.

Dodge, Andrew R., Betty K. Koed, and United States Congress Joint Committee on Printing, eds. *Biographical Directory of the United States Congress, 1774–2005: The Continental Congress, September 5, 1774, to October 21, 1788, and the Congress of the United States, from the First through the One Hundred Eighth Congresses, March 4, 1789, to January 3, 2005, Inclusive.* Washington, DC: US GPO, 2005.

Du Fossat, Elve Anna Bowie Moore Soniat. *Biographical Sketches of Louisiana's Governors: From D'Iberville to McEnery, by a Louisianaise, as a Contribution to the Exhibit of Woman's Work, in the Louisiana State Department, at the World's Industrial and Cotton Centennial Exposition, New Orleans, La., 1884–85.* New York: A. W. Hyatt, 1885.

Eaton, Dorothy S. "Introduction to the Index to the George Washington Papers, Microfilm Collection." Library of Congress, 1964. https://www.loc.gov/collections/george-washington-papers/articles-and-essays/provenance/.

Ecker, Grace Dunlop. *A Portrait of Old Georgetown.* Richmond, VA: Garrett and Massie, 1933.

Elliott, Stephen. "Address of the Rt. Reverend Stephen Elliott, D.D., to the Thirty-Ninth Annual Convention of the Protestant Episcopal Church of the Diocese of Georgia." Savannah, GA: John M. Cooper & Co., 1861.

Ferslew, W. Eugene. *Vickery's Directory of the City of Norfolk.* Norfolk, VA: Vickery, 1860.

"Floricultural Intelligence: New Seedling Camellias." In *The Magazine of Horticulture, Botany, and All Useful Discoveries and Improvements in Rural Arts,* vol. 8, edited by C. M. Hovey, 173–75. Boston: Hovey & Co., 1842.

Franz, Edgar. *Philipp Franz Von Siebold and Russian Policy and Action on Opening Japan in the Middle of the Nineteenth Century.* Munich: Iudicium, 2005.

Goode, James M. *Capital Losses: A Cultural History of Washington's Destroyed Buildings.* Washington, DC: Smithsonian Institution Press, 2003.

Gordon, William A. "Old Homes on Georgetown Heights." *Records of the Columbia Historical Society* 18 (1915): 70–91.

Gouverneur, Marian Campbell. *As I Remember: Recollections of American Society during the Nineteenth Century.* New York: D. Appleton, 1911.

Grimmett, Richard. *St. John's Church, Lafayette Square: The History and Heritage of the Church of the Presidents, Washington, DC.* Minneapolis, MN: Mill City, 2009.

Haley, Kenneth C. "A Nineteenth Century Portraitist and More: James Alexander Simpson." *Maryland Historical Magazine* 72, no. 3 (Fall 1977): 401–12.

Hamersly, Lewis R. *The Records of Living Officers of the U.S. Navy and Marine Corps, with a History of Naval Operations during the Rebellion of 1861–5.* Vol. 2. Philadelphia: J. B. Lippincott, 1870.

Harp, Jamalin Rae. "The Capital's Children: The Story of the Washington City Orphan Asylum, 1815–1860." Master's thesis, Texas Christian University, 2012.

Harrison, Eliza Cope, ed. *Best Companions: Letters of Eliza Middleton Fisher and Her Mother, Mary Hering Middleton, from Charleston, Philadelphia, and Newport, 1839–1846.* Columbia: University of South Carolina Press, 2001.

Hart, Charles Henry. "Gilbert Stuart's Portraits of Women: Elizabeth Beale Bordley (Mrs. James Gibson)." *Century Magazine* 55, no. 1 (November 1897): 151.

———. "Original Portraits of Washington, including Hitherto Unpublished Portraits of General and Mrs. Washington and Nelly Custis." *Century Magazine* 43 (February 1892): 593–99.

———. "Some New Washington Relics, I. from the Collection of Mrs. B. W. Kennon." *Century Magazine* 40, no. 1 (May 1890): 14–22.

Harte, N. B. "The British Linen Trade with the United States in the Eighteenth and Nineteenth Centuries." Paper presented at the Textiles in Trade: Proceedings of the Textile Society of America Biennial Symposium. September 14–16, 1990. Washington, DC.

Hibben, Henry B. *Navy-Yard, Washington, History from Organization, 1799 to Present Date.* Washington, DC: US GPO, 1890.

Historic American Landscape Survey, Theodore Roosevelt Island, HALS No. DC-12. Washington, DC: National Park Service, US Department of the Interior, n.d.

Historical Records Survey of Virginia Service Division and the Works Projects Administration. *Index to Marriage Notices in the Southern Churchman, 1835–1941.* 1942. Reprint, Baltimore, MD: Clearfield, 1996.

Hovey, C. M., ed. *The Magazine of Horticulture, Botany, and All Useful Discoveries and Improvements in Rural Affairs.* Vol. 8. Boston: Hovey & Co., 1842.

Hudson, Mark. "For the Inspiration of the People of the United States: Tudor Place's Scenic Easement at 50." *Tudor Place Times,* Spring 2016, p. 1–2. http://tudorplace.org/wp-content/uploads/2017/06/TudorNLSpring-April-2016.pdf.

Hunter, Alfred. *The Washington and Georgetown Directory, Stranger's Guidebook for Washington, and Congressional and Clerk's Register.* Washington, DC: Kirkwood & McGill, 1853.

Huntington, Frances Carpenter. "The Heiress of Washington City: Marcia Burnes Van Ness, 1782–1832." *Records of the Columbia Historical Society* 69/70 (1969): 80–101. www.jstor.org/stable/40067706.

Jackson, Donald, and Dorothy Twohig, eds. *The Diaries of George Washington.* Vol. 6, *January 1790–December 1799.* Charlottesville: University of Virginia Press, 1979.

Jackson, Richard Plummer. *The Chronicles of Georgetown, D.C., from 1751–1878.* Washington, DC: Polkinhorn, 1878.

Janke, Lucinda Prout. *A Guide to Civil War Washington, D.C.: The Capital of the Union.* Mount Pleasant, SC: Arcadia, 2013.

Johnson, Mary. "Madame Rivardi's Seminary in the Gothic Mansion." *Pennsylvania Magazine of History and Biography* 104, no. 1 (January 1980): 3–38.

Johnson, Robert Winder. *The Ancestry of Rosalie Morris Johnson, Daughter of George Calvert Morris and Elizabeth Kuhn, His Wife.* Philadelphia: Ferris & Leach, 1905.

Kail, Wendy. "George Washington's Great-Granddaughter and the Topographical Engineer: The Life and Times of William G. Williams, Class of 1824." *Assembly* 57, no. 6 (July/August 2000): 52–57.

———. "Oakland: Far from the Madding Crowd." March 2016. https://tudorplace.org/wp-content/uploads/2016/04/Oakland-March-2016_revised.pdf.

———. "On the Track—Thomas Peter, Henry Clay, and the Duchess of Marlborough." September 2013. https://tudorplace.org/wp-content/uploads/2013/12/On-the-Track-essay.pdf.

———. "Tudor Place and the Civil War Home Front: Britannia Leaves Tudor Place." 2013. http://www.tudorplace.org/wp-content/uploads/2019/10/Civil-War-Years-FINAL-for-web.pdf.

———. "The Residence on H Street: Mrs. General Hamilton." February 2019. http://www.tudorplace.org

/wp-content/uploads/2019/02/HStreet-NW-11.28.2018
-jw_edited.pdf.

———. "War of 1812: Friends and Family." 2012. http://
www.tudorplace.org/wp-content/uploads/2013/12/War-of
-1812.pdf.

Karlin, Elyse Zorn, and Yvonne Markowitz. "The Story
behind the Martha Custis Pocket Watch." *Adornment, the
Magazine of Jewelry & Related Arts* 6, no. 1 (2007).

Katzman, David M. *Seven Days a Week: Women and Domestic
Service in Industrializing America*. Urbana: University of
Illinois Press, 1981.

Keller, Kate Van Winkle. "Pierre Landrin DuPort." In
American National Biography. Edited by John A. Garraty
and Mark C. Carnes. 24 vols. New York: Oxford
University Press, 1999.

Lallou, William J. "The Vaults in St. John's Churchyard,
Thirteenth Street above Chestnut, Philadelphia." *Records
of the American Catholic Historical Society of Philadelphia*
23, no. 4 (December 1912): 212–48.

Lane, Janie Warren Hollingsworth. *Key and Allied Families*
Macon, GA: J. W. Burke & Co., 1931. Reprint, Baltimore:
Clearfield, for Genealogical Publishing Company, 2009.

Lathrop, George Parsons, and Rose Hawthorne Lathrop.
*A Story of Courage: Annals of the Georgetown Convent of
the Visitation of the Blessed Virgin Mary*. Cambridge, MA:
Riverside Press, 1894.

Lawrence, Henry W. *City Trees: A Historical Geography
from the Renaissance through the Nineteenth Century*.
Charlottesville: University of Virginia Press, 2008.

Lebovich, Bill. "The Bodisco House (Clement Smith
House)." Written Historical and Descriptive Data,
Historic American Buildings Survey, HABS No. DC-174.
Washington, DC: National Park Service, US Department
of the Interior, 1999.

———. "Cooke's Row Villa No. 7." Written Historical and
Descriptive Data, Historic American Buildings Survey,

HABS DC-829. Washington, DC: National Park Service,
US Department of the Interior, 2000.

———. "Dumbarton Oaks." Written Historical and
Descriptive Data, Historic American Buildings Survey,
HABS No. DC-825. Washington, DC: National Park
Service, US Department of the Interior, 1999.

———. "The Laird-Dunlop-Lincoln House." Written
Historical and Descriptive Data, Historic American
Buildings Survey, HABS No. DC-630. Washington, DC:
National Park Service, US Department of the Interior,
1999.

Lesko, Kathleen Menzie, Valerie Babb, and Carroll R.
Gibbs. *Black Georgetown Remembered: A History of Its
Black Community from the Founding of "The Town of
George" in 1751 to the Present Day*. Washington, DC:
Georgetown University Press, 1991.

Levasseur, Auguste. *Lafayette in America in 1824 and 1825:
Journal of a Voyage to the United States*, translated by Alan
R. Hoffman. Manchester, NH: Lafayette Press, 2006.

Leisenring, L. Morris. "Hayes Manor." Written Historical
and Descriptive Data, Historic American Buildings
Survey, HABS No. MD-202. Washington, DC: National
Park Service, US Department of the Interior, 1961.

Lewis, Charlene M. Boyer. *Ladies and Gentlemen on Display:
Planter Society at the Virginia Springs*. Charlottesville:
University of Virginia Press, 2001.

Lillard, Stewart. *Here Come the Russians: The Diplomatic
Visits to the United States by the Ministers Plenipotentiary
(and Later Ambassadors) of the Russian Empire*. n.p.: Lulu
Press, 2017.

Lomax, Elizabeth Lindsay. *Leaves from an Old Washington
Diary, 1854–1863*. Edited by Lindsay Lomax Wood. New
York: Dutton, 1943.

Lossing, Benson J. *Mount Vernon and Its Associations:
Historical Biographical and Pictorial*. New York: W. A.
Townsend & Co., 1859.

Grant S. Quertermous is the curator and director of collections for the Classical American Homes Preservation Trust. As the former curator of Tudor Place Historic House and Garden, he spent five years researching the Peter family and using the collection to interpret their ownership of the National Historic Landmark property in Georgetown. He has appeared on C-SPAN and lectures frequently about the Peter family and the Tudor Place collection.